GROWING UP
IN
PLAIN VIEW

Stories of Plainview, Nebraska
in the '30's and '40's

by

Walter E. Sehnert

Copywrite © 1996
Walter E. Sehnert

Printed in the USA by

*M*ORRIS
PUBLISHING

3212 E. Hwy 30
Kearney, NE 68847
800-650-7888

INTRODUCTION

When my granddaughter, Sarah Messinger, asked me to tell her a story about when I was a little boy, I'm sure she never imagined the outpouring of memories which follow in this book. The stories by no means constitute a history of Plainview during this period of time. They deal only with my impressions of the people, and the events I experienced. It has been a very pleasurable journey for me to revisit the Plainview of my youth, to think about that place then, the people I knew, the things that went on at that time, more than a half century ago.

I hope that these stories will help Sarah and others to understand, a little, of the things that helped to shape the future of people of my generation, who grew up in a small midwestern town in that era.

The stories about Plainview were published first in the <u>Plainview News</u>, as occasional columns beginning in 1992. The history of the Nebraska Cornhusker football team was expanded from a speech given to the McCook Rotary Club.

For the most part, these stories and people and places are true. I would say that they were all true, but from a distance of more than 50 years I can't be entirely sure. As Mark Twain said, "I remember everything perfectly, whether it happened or not." So, dear reader, if you remember things differently, you no doubt are correct, and I apologize.

WS

DEDICATION

This book is sincerely dedicated to my father, Walter M. Sehnert and to the memory of my mother, Lenita Ackerman Sehnert and to the people of Plainview. No boy could have had a finer place in which to spend his formative years.

WS

ACKNOWEDGEMENTS

I would like to give thanks to Leonald Warneke of the Plainview News for giving voice to these columns in his newspaper; to the many people in Plainview who have answered my questions and helped me fix dates and details; to Sue Watts and the folks at McCook College who helped in the organization of this book, and guidance through the mysteries of the computer; and to my wife, Jean, for her willingness to read and correct manuscripts, make suggestions, and offer encouragement for this project.

WS

FORWARD

"Growing Up In Plain View" had its start several years ago when Walter Sehnert was captivated by a granddaughter's plea to "tell me about when you were a young boy." The reminiscing began and Sehnert, in semi-retirement, and with an inbred ability to use the pen, thought he would put some of the reminiscences to black on white. His next step was to submit them to the home-town newspaper. That newspaper's first reaction was "we'll take them and use them as space is available" and thought they might be satisfactory filler.

That attitude quickly changed. The articles were well-received by the newspaper's readers. Soon, the articles weren't filler, but used as soon as possible after receipt. The comments from readers were many and favorable.

Collecting these and other articles into one volume, provides the reader with, as was described by one of them, "a story that reads like a Norman Rockwell painting." That could not be more accurate. While the stories generally concern the people, places and events in Plainview, Nebraska, and of course, draw excellent interest from residents who were in the community in the 30's and 40's, even members of the younger generation and non-Plainviewites are finding the incidents and memories to be enjoyable reading. It makes them think of, and envy, the good life in Small Town, America.

The gift of writing to provide enjoyable reading comes naturally to the author. His mother, the late Lenita Sehnert, was this publisher's high school journalism teacher and later wrote articles for him in her home-town newspaper under the title, "Our Town." She must have inspired her son.

We think you'll find the colorful descriptions of "Growing Up In Plain View" to be enjoyable reading, whether you have Plainview connections or not.

Lee Warneke, publisher, The Plainview News

CONTENTS

Page

GROWING UP IN PLAINVIEW

A PLAINVIEW CHRISTMAS STORY

During the 30's, my Dad worked out an arrangement with a Mr. Riley, of Pierce, who had quite a large herd of Shetland ponies, and found them expensive to feed year around. Dad agreed to take one of the ponies, keep him through the winter, and in lieu of cash, trade a certain amount of baked goods for the pony.

The first pony that we got was black and white and we named him Flash. He was anything but Flash. He was shaped like a barrel, to the extent that it was hard to hang on with short legs. This was a real problem, since we always rode bareback. But the worst drawback to Flash was that he was mean and stubborn, and had no use for 10 year olds. I always had to have help getting a bridle in place, and even after getting aboard for a ride it was a constant battle of wills as to where or if we would go.

One time we were in the vacant lot in back of our house. There were perhaps eight of the neighborhood kids on hand, and with the usual difficulty I had gotten Flash bridled and had taken him for a short ride. Things seemed to be going well. Don Cline arrived with Gayety, his saddle horse, which Don claimed had been a race horse. Now, however, Gayety mainly walked, no doubt due to his 26 years. We had plannned to take a long ride (meaning several blocks, maybe all the way to College Addition and back). But first some of the kids wanted to

1

take a ride on the pony. Joanie was already an accomplished horsewoman, and had no trouble handling a slightly headstrong Shetland pony. But difficulty arose when Jayne took her turn. The pony seemed to sense that she was not only inexperienced, but also apprehensive, and he was skittish as we proceeded to lead him around the lot. Soon Jayne felt sure enough to have us give her the reins so that she could be in full control. This was a mistake.

As soon as we let go, Flash began to buck, which we had not seen before. To her credit, Jayne tried to stay with him, all the while crying "Whoa", and pulling on the reins. But it was no contest, and after only three or four bucks with a full spin, Jayne flew off. She made a perfect back flip, landing in a sitting position, in a spot used by Flash only a short time before. I can still hear my sister, Judy, running to the house, screaming, "Momma, Jayney got bucked off in the banure, Jayney got bucked off in the banure!"

Fortunately, Jayne was unhurt, physically. Her pride was another matter, and she lost no time beating it for home, and a complete change of clothes.

After this incident my mother put her foot down and announced that Flash was more than we could handle and he would have to go. So back to Mr. Riley my Dad went. This time he traded for a Shetland pony named Nicky. I'm sure that he had to pay more money, but whatever he paid, it was worth it. Nicky was a jewel. He was dark brown in color, with a darker mane. He was sleek and slender and ran like the wind. His crowning feature was that he had a good disposition, and seemed to love 10 year old boys and girls as much as we all loved him.

One of the girls in the neighborhood was Joanna, a dark haired, dark eyed beauty, one or two years younger than I. She was very pale and quiet, but she loved horses, and when we were out riding, she would always be close by, watching. Often we would see her go to the park across the street from our house, where Nicky was picketed, with a lump of sugar or an apple for treats. She loved to pet him, and nuzzle his ears, and talked softly to him while she straightened out his mane and tail. Since she did not run and play much, and was rarely out of sight of her mother, she was not really a part of the gang, but we all recognized her as being someone who found horses special.

That summer Joanna got terribly sick. We never knew just what her illness was, but on at least two occasions her mother called us into the house to visit Joanna and to try to cheer her up. This proved to be quite an ordeal because Joanna was confined to her bed, in a cast to her hips, which caused her her to be immobile, with her legs spread apart. Her disease must have been of the bone because there was a hole in the cast that allowed for drainage, and the discharge caused a terrible stench that almost gagged you as you stepped into the room.

After the first visit to Joanna's I announced to my mother that I would never go back. Mom vowed that I not only would go back on a regular basis, but I would take Joanna little gifts, and I would smile and cheer her as best I could. I can't say that I ever got so I enjoyed the visits, but I did go from time to time, and Joanna and I got to be friends.

Her parents did their best to be cheerful and encouraged us to come back often. Joanna's dad was always making jokes when he was around, and he did his best to include us and Joanna, whom he called "Princess", into his stories, trying to make her smile. However, that summer there were few smiles from Joanna, and even when she was well enough to be carried to the front porch it was only when I stopped by on Nicky that she would manage a little grin. At these times she would call to her mother to bring a little treat for Nicky, then smile broadly as he accepted it with enthusiasm.

Summer turned to fall, and with the demands of school I didn't see Joanna often, only occasionally when I rode by on Nicky and she happened to be on the porch or at the window. Then she would give us a friendly wave and smile. While she was still unable to attend school for the fall semester, she was improving and the cast had been pared down so that she could sit in a chair.

When the weather was crisp and the leaves were starting to fall, my Dad got us busy on another project. While we usually rode Nicky bareback, Dad had also picked up a small two wheeled cart, with harness, and we wondered how Nicky would take to being a driving horse. We needn't have worried. Mr. Riley's ponies all were broken to harness, and Nicky really enjoyed pulling that cart. Those early months of autumn were great. We had fun pretending that the cart was actually a racing sulky and that we were driving for a trotting horse championship, against the great trotting horse, Dan Patch.

One day Dad called me outside to see his latest acquisition. He had picked up a one horse cutter (sleigh) from Charlie Seabury, one that the Seabury family had brought from Canada years before. It was not in very good shape, but Dad assured me that by the time the snow flew we would have a one horse sleigh that we would be proud of, and gliding over the snow in that cutter would be the most fun of all.

I'm sure if he would have known (or more to the point, if my mother would have known) the trouble and expense that restoring that cutter brought he would have thanked Mr. Seabury very much for the kind thought and left the cutter on Mr. Seabury's farm. But no one knew, and things just got out of hand gradually.

Restoring that cutter really became sort of community project. Mr. Hoffart and the boys at the lumber yard repaired a broken shaft. Karl Malstrom, the blacksmith, manufactured a new runner which had to curve back upon itself in the front. The new runner turned out so well that he decided that he'd better put a new one on the other side as well. The boys in the body shop at Saathoff's Chevrolet garage painted the cutter a bright cherry red, and trimmed it in black. The upholsterer at the Boyens' furniture store put a new leatherette covering on the seat. And finally, Bob Johnson, at the harness shop, restrung the sleigh bells on a new flexible piece of harness that was custom fit just for Nicky. All of these people were as proud of the new cutter as we were and insisted that we must come around for an inspection the first time that we were out for a ride.

That year it seemed as if it would never snow, and it was near Christmas before enough snow had accumulated so that we could take a ride in the new cutter. Nicky was hitched to the sleigh, and the sleigh bells were in place. I really believe that Nicky thought we had brought this present just for him. He seemed to grow taller when he pulled that sleigh and held his head high and pranced to the sound of the bells. It was as if he were a one entry parade.

After a few preliminary passes around the block my mother called me over and suggested that Joanna might enjoy seeing the new cutter and Nicky in his finery, and just maybe she might be able to take a little ride. I'm sure that she must have been on the telephone to Joanna's mother, because when we got to Joanna's place a few minutes later Joanna was already in her snow suit and sitting on the porch waiting. Her father carried her to the curb, and after she had whispered a few words of endearment to Nicky, he lifted her into the sleigh. She still had a cast on, so that she could not bend her leg, but we managed to place her so that her leg could be inside the sleigh and covered with the warm comforter we were using.

By this time it was near 5 o'clock in the evening and at that time of the year it was almost dark. But we proceded with our ride none-the-less. To say that Joanna was thrilled is a understatement. I had never seen her so animated, and she almost sang with delight. Each house that we passed, which was decorated with holiday lights, brought squeals of appreciation. I began to get into the spirit as well, and told her about one house or another that had really outstanding lights or decorations, and we would ride by to see. Before we knew it we were at the highway, the business district, with its colored lights, decorations, and Christmas music, on the other side. I knew my mother, and certainly Joanna's mother, would not want us to go into the business district with the sleigh and pony, fearing the automobile traffic. But by this time we were having so much fun, and no one was coming, so across the highway we went, into the heart of

Plainview, to make a complete circuit of the two blocks of Locust Street, the main business section.

You would have thought that Santa himself had come to call. Cars pulled to the side of the street for us to pass, and everyone called out "Merry Christmas" and waved. Clerks and customers came to the front of the stores to see what sort of parade was going by. Many people recognized Joanna and called to her by name and said how good it was to see her. She beamed at everyone, and as she called my attention to yet another wonderful decoration in one of the stores, turned to me and said with a lilt in her voice and a tear in her eye,

"Today, I truly do feel like a Princess, and this is my fairy kingdom. And this is my magic sleigh. Thank you very very much. This is going to be my best Christmas ever."

Eat It Up, Wear It Out, Make It Do

My mother, Lenita Ackerman Sehnert, was a teacher. She considered teaching the most noble of callings. She taught, formally, for only two short periods, four years in the Presho, SD, high school in the 20's (where she met my father), and again for four years at the Osmond High School, during the war. However, she spent her entire life teaching, in one form or another.

She taught Sunday School for many years at the Plainview Congregational Church, where she used a variety of innovative ways to help us learn the biblical stories. Once the Council Oak Store was able to obtain a special order of pomegranates, so that we might sample the unfamiliar (to us) fruit so frequently mentioned in the bible.

Louise Bradley says that when Lenita found out that some of the young ladies in town wanted to learn to play bridge, she organized an informal class at our apartment, and these young women had fun learning a game they could enjoy for the rest of their lives.

When the bakery began to make colored bread, Lenita instructed to ladies at most of the churches in the art of making fancy, tasty sandwiches, using bread in the bride's colors.

Teaching someone to drive requires a special talent. My father lacked the patience to teach my sister and me to drive, so in those pre "Driver's Training At School" days, that chore fell to Lenita, who not only taught us to drive, but helped a number of women in the community to gain greater independence, by teaching them to drive a car.

During the last years of her life Lenita attempted to teach the people of Plainview, by pointing out the danger we all faced from Big Government, and its fiscal irresponsibility, through her column, "Our Town", in the Plainview News (editor, Leonald Warneke, was one of her former students). Unfortunately, a good many of the dire consequences of our government's excesses that she predicted in her column are with us today.

When Lenita taught in the high schools, her main subjects were Latin and English. She considered Latin the foundation for a good education in English. Not only did it provide the basis for a good English vocabulary, it also provided the student with an appreciation for the beauty of the English language. She felt that a nation's people could be studied both through their history and their literature, but the study of literature was a lot more interesting.

I've always felt that Lenita's favorite Latin word must have been "consueri", meaning to take care of, to preserve. From this root word we derive "conservative", which certainly describes Lenita's political posture, but we also get "conservation" which describes her way of life. Her motto, which we heard again and again was "Eat it up. Wear it out. Make it do".

Today we pay great lip service to conservation, and think it's the "in" thing to do, to take care of the "environment", so we recycle plastic, even while we diaper our young in Pampers and groom our lawns with insecticides, weed killers, fertilizer, gas driven mowers, and great quantities of water.

Conservation and recycling is not a new concept. In the depression 30's, and all the generations before, everyone was a conservationist, by necessity. Money was in short supply and many people suffered terribly from its lack. Some complained bitterly of its lack during that entire period, and some saw its lack as a challenge. Lenita fell into the latter group.

<u>Eat it up</u>. At the table, food had to be eaten up completely, else it would come back the next day in a new form. We ate a lot of bread pudding, which I usually didn't mind because her bread pudding really was delicious, except at Christmas time, when those red and green scraps of bread from the fancy sandwiches added a bit more color than I liked.

In the days when Lenita worked regularly at the bakery she frequently utilized the bakery oven which retained heat throughout the day. A roast, with a variety of vegetables, became a very tasty meal by the end of her shift, a bit like making dinner in the world's largest crock pot.

Being a food recycler meant that Lenita made a lot of soup, and while the soup might start out to be Vegetable, or Chili, or Chicken, in truth it would turn out to be whatever she could retrieve from the refrigerator. We put our foot down, though, and refused to eat the soup the time she put lettuce and radishes into the mixture. In the cooking process those items became transparent and a bit slimy and singularly unappetizing.

While we never did raise much of a garden we did trade baked goods for fresh vegetables, so Lenita canned fruits and vegetables for our table. In the 30's, before spraying the ditches became common, we also picked asparagus, chokecherries, grapes, and plums along the country roads.   Jellies and jams from those fruits were great favorites.

Wear it out. Lenita hadn't done much sewing as a girl, but with the help of some older friends, she became quite an adequate seamstress after she moved to Plainview.   She never did consider herself proficient enough to make things for my Dad and me, except for the aprons she made out of flour sacks for the bakery. But she sewed extensively for my sister, very often using her old dresses for material, and even using my dad's old suits to make skirts and vests.   Once, when a certain garment had been recycled for the 3rd or 4th time, my sister cried out in exasperation, "Mom, you just don't recognize when something is really worn out!"

Make it do. On the subject of money, Lenita stressed, repeatedly, that:

1. We must always live within our means. I'm sure that she never did use a credit card.

2. We were expected to work for what we got, that no honest work was degrading, but once we accepted a job we must strive to do it to the best of our ability.

3. From each paycheck we must save a little. She said that a common fault with people was that they thought that if they couldn't save a lot then saving was not worthwhile. "Not so!", she preached. "If you can't save a dollar, at least save a nickel or a penny. The pennies and nickels will grow to be dollars."

Lenita thought that many people lived too extravagantly, but also spent needlessly, without raising their standard of living. When you left a room and left the light on that was waste. "You don't work for the power company. Turn out the light!" In this regard she

11

was not as strict as some. My mother-in-law told of living with her grandmother as a child. Her grandmother had it figured, exactly, just how much they could use lights each night and still stay under the minimum electric bill. In December that meant either not using lights at all after the evening meal, or preparing supper, eating, and cleaning up in the dark so that the two hours of light could be used for reading later in the evening.

For a long time Lenita thought about the beautiful cards that came at Christmas time. She had saved several large boxes of cards when she came up with the idea of re-using them in the form of name tags, to be used for parties, or on Christmas gifts (today that is another form of recycling). She would cut out a scene, or part of scene with her pinking shears, then fasten that to a somewhat larger card with glue or ribbon, creating an entirely new card. Soon she had them in many forms, small, for bridge tallies, medium for package identifiers, and very often an entirely new card. They were much appreciated, to the extent that she began giving boxes of her new creations to family members and friends on birthdays.

In the basement of our house Lenita had her treasure chest of empty boxes. When boxes of any size came into the house, instead of throwing them out when empty, she sorted them into sizes, so that whenever anyone needed a box, of any size, he was very likely to find it downstairs, along with wrapping paper and string salvaged from former packages.

Again, in the matter of saving things Lenita was not unusual, or even as determined as many people of the 30's. It was a way of life. A friend tells of her grandmother who lived alone, on a fixed income. She saved string, bacon grease, yard goods, everything. In those days peaches, by the lug, came individually wrapped in orange tissue paper. This lady saved the paper, ironed it flat, then stacked it in the bathroom, in lieu of toilet paper. She only half-soled shoes once. After that she used a bit of cardboard inside the shoe to squeeze out a few more miles.

Today I know of no one who darns socks. Probably the use of the synthetic yarns in socks means that socks do not wear out in the heel like they did years ago. Never-the-less, one of my recollections is that of my mother sitting in her chair, rocking, and darning socks, while we all listened to our favorite radio shows, helping us to get a few extra miles out our socks.

Lenita's love for conserving things led naturally to the collection of antiques. Over the years she bought numerous old objects she considered valuable. After one or two projects of refinishing furniture items she confined her collection to small china and glass items. She gleaned the library for information on the history of these items and over time gained a reputation for her knowledge of the market value of various classes of antiques. Her collection, housed in the upstairs of our home, was a regular stop for prominent antique dealers from out of state, who regularly visited, to talk shop, and buy and sell various objects of interest.

Her collection of bread plates gained her a great deal of respect from knowledgeable antique dealers, but with the exception of duplicates, no bread plate was ever for sale.

I am sure that the conserving of the beautiful old items was always her goal, rather than the profit that could be made from their sale, though to justify her hobby she frequently referred to the value of these items.

One story that we never did let her live down, concerned the purchase of a dish which she uncovered in a box of miscellany from a yard sale. She was elated over the discovery, when she reported to us, "I only paid fifty cents for the entire box, and that one dish, why it's **priceless.** I know that I would have no trouble selling it for $25!"

So, what would Lenita think if she could know that her way of life, involving saving, recycling, and avoidance of waste is now popular, and is the "in thing" to do as we approach the new century? I think she would say, "Wonderful! Its a great idea that makes sense--and dollars."

Learning Right and Correcting Wrong

In the days before WWII, when my father and mother had the bakery on the south side of Locust Street in Plainview (the building now occupied by Barbara Young's Antique Store), we parked the bakery delivery truck in a narrow space between the bakery and Goos' grocery store next door. This made it quite handy to load the truck for deliveries, since we did not have to carry the boxes of bread and trays of rolls all the way to the alley. Also, the truck did not have to be parked in the alley, and it was assumed that this provided a bit of protection for the vehicle.

One time, however, Merton Grecow, the delivery man at the time, noticed that when he would leave cigarettes or candy, or loose change in the glove compartment of the truck over the weekend, these items would invariable be gone on Monday, when the truck was loaded for the first delivery. Of course the truck was never locked up when it was put away. In those days few people in Plainview locked their cars, or houses for that mater. It was taken for granted that one respected the property rights of others. This, in fact, was drilled into me at a very early age.

We were living in an apartment above the bakery at the time. I came home, one day, eating an apple. When my mother asked me where I had gotten the apple, I admitted that I had taken it, without paying, from an apple display in front of Houston's store, across the street from the bakery. My mother immediately lectured me on the evils of stealing, and to emphacize the point, she marched me across the street to the store, paid the clerk for the apple, and made me apologize for my crime. The clerk tried to smooth the whole thing over and said that it was all right and that I could just have the apple.

"He will assuredly **not** have the apple", she replied. And off home again we went, the apple lying, half eaten, on the counter. I realized that this was really a serious matter, as my mother was from the school whose motto was "Waste Not-Want Not", and that certainly was a perfectly good apple which we had left on the counter.

Apparently the lesson sank in, because my mother told of a time shortly after this; I was walking up the street with my friend, Ben Saunders, the banker. He looked down and spotted a very pretty marble lying on the sidewalk, and said to me,

"Look, Walt, there's a marble for you".
I walked over, picked it up, looked it over closely.

"Nope, it's not one of mine", I said, and carefully put it back on the sidewalk for the real owner to claim. So much for my early training on property rights.

This mystery of the missing truck items had gone on for two or tree weeks when I overheard Merton Grecow telling my Dad about the trouble.

"I sure would like to know who is getting into our truck. I'd give that so and so a lesson he'd not soon forget!" And he continued with more threats of that sort. They talked it over for a few minutes more and then I suppose they forgot about it until the next time we were robbed. But I couldn't forget about it. After all, I was a regular at the Saturday matinees, and like Tom Mix and Tailspin Tommy , of the movies, I was a man of action, or at least I romanticized that I was. And what's more, I thought that I could catch our burglar.

16

By the end of the week I had formulated my plan of attack. Prudently, however, I decided to take my Dad into my confidence, and told him how I thought we might catch the thief. He listened, but was skeptical. I was insistent, so he finally agreed that I might try my plan out, but I had to promise that I would not apprehend anyone by myself, but merely give the signal, and wait for help. I agreed and could hardly wait for the time to put the plan into action.

My plan was to climb a large elm tree across the alley from the bakery on the next Saturday night, and watch for the burglar from a sort of platform that we boys had wedged between a couple of the tree's branches. When and if I saw anyone approach the truck from the alley I was to give the signal and the people from inside the bakery would make tha actual citizen's arrest.

I had gone into the tree just after dark, which at that time of the year seemed to be about 9 or 9:30 at night. I waited and waited. The platform, which seemed to be very spacious and comfortable when we were playing in the tree, now was very narrow and hard, and extremely uncomfortable. It was cold and I was getting sleepy. After what seemed an awfully long time, sure enough, someone did come down the alley--two men. They didn't act very mysterious, as they kept up their conversation about the economy and farming in general. They came right up to the tree where I was hiding.

I held my breath. I surely didn't want them to see me, no matter what they were looking for. It soon became apparent that they were not looking for anyone or anything, but were merely taking a breather from the pool hall, and had chosen my tree as the place to relieve themselves. Such indignity! But they didn't look up. I

17

didn't make any noise, and they soon made their way back from whence they had come.

So I waited some more, and became more cold and uncofortable in my cramped space. I was ready to give up my quest as a bad idea when I became aware of someone slipping around the corner of the grocery store, very close to the wall and into the space beside the bakery truck. He went slowly, but deliberately, directly up to the door of the truck's cab. I heard the truck door open and I gave the signal for the people in the bakery to come. The signal we had agreed upon was the bob-white bird whistle. We had all agreed that the bob-white call was really not appropriate at night, but since this was the only bird call I knew, it would have to do. I whistled, slowly and softly at first, then with more insistance. But no one came. As I learned later, everyone at the bakery had gotten busy with other things and had long ago left their stations where they could have heard the signal. I repeated my bird call again and again, but to no avail.

I imagined that the thief was taking everything out of the truck, including the seats and transmission, and I got mad. Mad at the thief, at the people at the bakery, at everyone. I would have made the arrest myself, but by this time my imagination had gotten the best of me, and I was afraid that he might have a knife or a gun.

I wanted to throw something, but had long since eaten the apple that I had brought with me, and that was the only weapon that I had. Finally, in sheer desperation to do something, anything, I took off my shoe, and balancing as best I could in my treetop perch, I hurled the shoe against the back of the bakery truck. I got a lucky throw, and it did make the loudest bang there in the dark, still night.

It did the trick too, as the thief come out of the truck, and out into the alley as fast as an overweight, slightly crippled, 70 year old man can move. He didn't know where the shoeshot had come from, and really did not wait around to investigate. As he came hurrying away from the truck (running would be too strong a term), he passed directly beneath my treetop observation post. I had no trouble identifying the culprit as Bill K., a shiftless, harmless, character around town, whose round form and shuffling gate were as distinctive as his peculiar, pungent smell which followed him out of the alley.

Stiffly, I climbed down from my perch and hobbled to the truck, found my shoe, and went into the bakery to report the solving of the mystery. I was all for getting the night marshall at once, to have him arrest Bill K. and lock him up in the (light plant) jail.

My Dad got me calmed down after a bit and suggested that we talk about it at Bartlett's Drug Store. He allowed that we might have a bit of trouble proving that Bill K. was the thief, since we did not actually catch him in the act. All we could say with certainty was that the culprit **smelled** like Bill K., and it would come down to his word against mine. He really did not want to subject me to a confrontation of that kind. He appreciated my efforts in solving the case, but thought that, just maybe, we might be better off locking the truck in the future, and not saying anything to anyone about it. I grumbled a bit more, but his argument carried great weight as we sipped our ice cream sodas, and I finally agreed to chalk the whole thing up as a great "moral" victory.

•

ONE OF LIFE'S LITTLE LESSONS

A good teacher, so they say, is someone who can present a subject in an interesting or unusual manner, in a way that will penetrate the consciousness of his pupils, and cause them to remember what it is that he is trying to teach. If this is indeed true, then Bob White is one of the greatest teachers I have known.

Bob White, whose folks operated the Corner Cafe in the early 30's, was three years older, and decades wiser than I. It always seemed to me that he patterned himself after Mickey Rooney, a popular "kid star" of the day. Both Bob and Mickey Rooney were short of stature and carried themselves with a definite swagger. Both were outwardly self assured, even a bit cocky, were quick with the quip, and definitely feisty. Also, like the Mickey Rooney character, Bob was friendly and likeable. As a small boy he displayed a talent for singing and dancing, and with his sister, Mickie, won a number of amateur contests, before he decided that such things were unmanly, and abruptly retired from a show business career. He had an active mind and was constantly thinking up things to do, things that sometimes got us into trouble.

At the Corner Cafe, about this time, there was a regular customer who fascinated all of us, but Bob and me in particular. He had a talent for rolling his own cigarettes, which at that time was not unusual; but his trick was that after sprinkling tobacco on the cigarette paper, he could roll the combination into an almost perfect cigarette, "using only one hand". He loved to perform this feat, and did it with great showmanship.

20

We longed to emulate his trick, but never did have the materials to try.

Mickie White, Betty Cox (whose mother cooked for the Whites at the Corner Cafe), and I were the same age, and since we were downtown a great deal of the time, we played together and became very good friends. One day Bob called Mickie, Betty and me aside and told us to meet him at the grove. He had something he wanted to show us.

At the end of Locust Street there was a small grove of trees, along the railroad tracks, where bums sometimes slept between trains. It was shady and cool in summer, and there were paths meandering among the trees. It was a fine place to track "wild animals" (rabbits), and to play hide and seek.

Someone had rigged up a rope swing in one of the trees, so we could practice our Tarzan yells and work off a good bit of energy, while we took turns on the swing.

When we got to the grove Bob produced a small pouch of tobacco, some cigarette papers and matches. He announced that he was going to teach us how to roll our own cigarettes, just like the fellow at the cafe. Of course our efforts were a joke, even with two hands. We either got too much tobacco, or could not get it distributed evenly. But Bob said that we should not worry. Those odd shapes were OK. He observed, "Those must be Camels!", which would account for the hump in the middle.

Finally we succeeded to the point where we could light up and smoke "our personally rolled cigarettes". I remember that they burned very fast and tasted awful. Bob asked us how we liked them, and not wanting to appear unsophisticated, we all agreed that they were

21

great. With that Bob started to laugh and said, "That wasn't really tobacco in that pouch. Har! Har! Har! What you were smoking was **dried horse manure!**" Whether it was or not I don't know. But my reaction was immediate and violent. I have never been so sick to my stomach since that time. And to this day smoking has never been one of my vices. After 60 years, my belated thanks to Bob White, Teacher 1st Class.

LIVING DOWNTOWN

In 1930 my folks, Walter and Lenita Sehnert, sold their bakery in Ft. Pierre, South Dakota, and on a tip from older brother, Dick Sehnert, visited the bakery in Plainview, owned by Sam Johnson. They liked the town, and liked the business. My Dad soon made the deal for the bakery purchase, and proceeded to move his family to Plainview. At that time family consisted of my father, my mother and me, age 2. My sister, Judy, was born at the Plainview hospital in 1931.

One of the features of the business deal that attracted my Dad was the apartment above the bakery in which they could live. Since that was the arrangement that his parents had had in Presho, SD, Dad thought this was a perfect situation, both from a convenience and an economic standpoint. After all, his parents had raised a family of eight in an apartment not too much bigger.

My mother was not as happy with the living quarters, and from the beginning looked upon them as being a temporary solution to their housing problem. If her dream was not exactly the proverbial white house with picket fence, at least she hoped someday to be able to take her family away from downtown Plainview.

From the beginning, I thought that downtown was the ideal place to live. We regularly walked to the library, to Chilver's Park, with its swings and merry-go-round, and the Congregational Church. And from a very early age I began to visit the bakery and other businesses in the downtown area. As I look back on this time it is hard for me to believe that those business men would take the time to visit with a youngster, but they did. I'm sure that business flowed at a slower pace in that depression era. And too, with Saturdays being so very important (probably two thirds of the week's business was done on that one day), there probably was more free time during the first part of the week for unproductive chit chat. At any rate, the banker, the butchers, the bakers, the people who worked at the stores, as well as the widow ladies who lived upstairs in the Frost Block, were all my early friends, and I visited them regularly.

There were also other kids downtown, much more so than is the case nowadays. Baby-sitters were not so common (no one had that extra money), so the owners and workers in the various stores frequently brought their offspring to work with them, and eventually we all got together to play.

One of the places that I liked to play was at the Gilster home, located south of the railroad tracks on West Street, across from the Sale Barn. There were several bigger boys in that family, and there were always animals, and interesting things to do on their acreage, or across the street at the sale barn where we attempted to practice our cowboy skills on the calves in the pens. My mother was not keen on my spending too much time with those boys as they delighted in helping me with my vocabulary. When I gushed forth with an endearment for my baby sister that they had taught me, I was quickly informed that those words should never be used, certainly not in polite company.

One of the few times I remember being spanked by my mother came as a result of a visit to the Gilsters. Somehow she found out that the train had blocked West street and wondered how I had gotten to their place and back. When I informed her that Hop Gilster and I merely crawled under the train to get to the other side

24

she turned pale, then got terribly angry and spanked me good. After that she held me tight and cried for a long time. I never took that short cut again. I'm sure that it must have been then that she made up her mind to move away from downtown.

Since Saturdays were such a busy day at the bakery, to keep out of the way, I regularly attended the matinee at the theater. This was one of the highlights of the week for me. There was usually a continued adventure story, called a serial, plus a cartoon, and sometimes a double feature, to make up the program. It kept me occupied for most of the afternoon. The shows I liked best were the westerns. Tom Mix, Buck Jones, and Ken Maynard were the stars that I, and most of the other boys my age, emulated. Tom Mix also had a radio program at that time for the Ralston Purina Company. On that show he regularly offered merchandise for Ralston boxtops and 10 or 15 cents in cash, so most of us sported sheriff badges, neck kerchiefs, and even toy six guns and holsters, endorsed by Tom.

For my seventh birthday my mother organized a great party. All of the boys in my class at school and all of my boy friends (no girls allowed) from downtown were invited, and all came in full cowboy regalia. A snapshot preserves the memory of 15 little boys in bandanas, chaps, and sombrero hats, all armed with six guns, looking very fierce before the camera.

The party took place on a Saturday afternoon, and of course we went to the matinee. It was an uproarious event. Members of the party were quick to warn Tom Mix of the bad guy who was sneaking up behind him, and when Tom finally won out in the end there were loud cheers from our section. Mrs. Huffman,

25

the proprietor's wife had to make at least two trips down the aisle to tell us to keep quiet.

After the movie we all adjourned to the alley behind the bakery to recreate the movie western for an hour before lunch. We took turns being Tom, or Buck, or Ken, or the bad guys, who had to die that agonizing death over and over.

In those days of the middle 30's we did not have a variety store as such, and no one had much money to spend, so birthday presents tended to be a little different than those now generally given. Typically, for a birthday, a boy might receive, among other things, a comb, a bottle of hair oil, a regular white handkerchief, a ruler, two pencils, a jar of homemade apple jelly, four stamps, packs of gum, and a package of sen sen. For my birthday I remember that I received most of these items plus some seventy five cents in nickels and dimes.

At that party we served cake that I had been allowed to make by myself at the bakery (with plenty of help from my father), along with homemade ice cream that we had cranked earlier in the day. I had also made another cake for my class at the school. For that one even the girls were invited to join in.

One of the memories from that party is that when all the guests had departed the seventy five cents had also disappeared from the table holding the gifts. I was devastated, and thought we should call the police, because I was sure I knew who had taken the money. My mother convinced me that we must let the matter drop, but suggested that perhaps I should not play any more with that boy (who later spent his career as an honest and successful law officer).

26

THE SAFARI

That summer we were known as the Four Musketeers. We had all recently seen a movie which covered some of the exploits of Dumas' famous trio. The way that the Musketeers mixed high fun and adventure with loyalty, and sticking by one's friends to the bitter end was very appealing and reminded us of the way we saw ourselves. It didn't take us long to adjust the title and adopt it for our own. But unlike the original Musketeers, who seemed to find adventure around every corner, we relied mainly on our collective imaginations to find excitement in Plainview during the years leading up to World War II.

It was one of those great, lazy days of summer, of which boyhood seems to be made. The other Musketeers and I were lounging in the park, trying to decide what to do. The conversation turned to a book that one of the guys had picked up at the library, one that covered a trip that Martin Johnson, the big game hunter and explorer, had made into the heart of Africa. Suddenly, an adventure of this sort seemed like the perfect project for this particular day.

In no time we had laid out the plans for our own safari. Africa was out as a destination, but a trip south of town on our bicycles was attractive, and though we did not have powerful big game rifles, we did all have BB guns, and for our own Big Game, this was all the fire power we would need. Except for Wayne.

Wayne was not a regular of our group, but he lived in the neighborhood and was frequently around when things were happening. Wayne was always aggressive, and sometimes a bit violent, but he was a good athlete, and took kidding well, so he was a fun fellow to have along, and we welcomed him on our trip.

We all beat it home for a little take along lunch and our air rifles. A little later, when we got together for the start of the trip, instead of the BB gun which we had expected, Wayne had brought along a 410 caliber shot gun, and pockets full of ammunition.

I believe everyone was a bit apprehensive concerning the shot gun. We were not especially fearful of the gun. It was more that we were put out over this bit of one-upmanship on Wayne's part. Finally, after a little grumbling, everyone accepted the shot gun, and the safari began.

We proceeded south, single file, out of town. We didn't really have a destination, but wanted to go as far as we could and still be back in time for supper. I remember hearing someone say that we could probably get 20 or 30 miles south before we would have to turn back.

At the mile point #1 and again at mile #3 we stopped in small groves to see what sort of game we could scare up. We saw squirrels and rabbits and birds in both groves and a couple of the boys managed to get a shot off before Wayne scared everything away with his 410. We yelled quite a bit at him for firing before the rest of us had chance to stalk the game. He said that he really didn't care to be a big game humter anyway. He was a law man and he was bringing in his quarry, dead or alive.

We actually did travel 5 or 6 miles south of town. Peddling on the gravel roads with a gun slung over our shoulders, in the heat, proved to be considerable work. We finally came on an abandoned farm stead, and convinced ourselves that this was our destination all along.

The farm yard was grown up into weeds, but the house and out-buildings seemed to be in pretty good shape. Everyone made a beeline for the pump in the yard, for a cool drink of water. Hank, assuming the role of leader, issued an order, that we should all stay together, and explore the out-buildings, one at a time, before we looked over the main house. So, of course, everyone headed in a different direction; to the barn, to the corn crib, to the outhouse, and I to the main house, to explore.

The house was locked, but a window over the cellar door was unlocked, and I had gained entrance in moments. The house was completely cleaned out. Even the stoves in the living room and kitchen were gone, though you could see where the stove pipes had fit into the chimneys. The house smelled a bit musty from being closed up, but not really bad. I poked into the downstairs rooms, which consisted of a large kitchen, front room, two small bedrooms, but no bathroom. Proceeding up the narrow stairway I found a central hallway, with a room on either side.

In one of the upstairs rooms, bare as the other rooms otherwise, was a picture of two horses, manes and tails flying, running along a road toward a copse of trees. The picture was in a large frame, and leaning against the wall, on the floor, as if ready to be carried out on the next load when they were dismantling the house. In the absence of anything else of interest, I felt that this constituted a discovery. I glanced out the window and saw that some of the guys were standing in the yard below. I tried to open the window so I could yell at them of my discovery, but the window was stuck.

I had just turned away from the window when "Wham!", a blast tore through the window and into the ceiling over my head. Plaster and lathe, and glass came down all around me, and the room was filled with dust. I was not hurt, but my knees shook badly, as I hurried down the stairs and out into the yard. Of course, it had been Wayne's 410 that had done the damage, and I tried to get that fact across, as I sputtered that I had been in that room when the shot came, and why hadn't he been more careful, and on and on. Wayne was calm about the whole incident, and said that he had seen something, maybe only a shadow in that room and he had supposed it to be an animal or bird of some sort and he thought he could get off a good shot. Almost too good!

It wasn't long before the incident was put behind us. After all, an adventure needs a little danger. Hank did take the precaution of collecting all the weapons and putting them in one place till we were ready to get on the road again.

One of the features of the farm that attracted our collective attention was a gigantic wood pile, located between the garage and the house. This wood pile was at least 20 feet long, and 4 1/2 to 5 feet high, and at least 5 feet wide. The wood was neatly stacked, and the pile really was in better shape than some of the out-buildings.

We had just started to examine the wood pile when a car roared into the driveway. A farmer jumped out and hurried toward us shouting that we were trespassing on his property and he was going to call the sheriff. I'm sure that everyone wanted to run, thinking of the shot out window, but it was too late, and we all just froze in our tracks awaiting the worst. Except for Wayne. He had already climbed on top of the wood pile and when the farmer came toward us, Wayne did run, and was gone. One moment he was atop the wood pile hurrying to get off, the next moment he was just gone, vanished. Then, from inside the wood pile, we heard, "Hey you guys, get me out of here!", and immediately, "Yeow!, There's mice down here. Gimme my shot gun, I'm gonna blast em!" Wayne had fallen inside the woodpile!

Everyone just stood still for the moment. Then some of us climbed on the wood pile to give Wayne a hand. But the farmer surprised us. He ordered Wayne to stay where he was. He ran back to the car. When he rejoined us, monents later, he handed a flashlight to Wayne and instructed him to tell us everything he saw inside the woodpile.

Wayne looked around a bit, and said that it was empty in there, except for a broken bottle which he tossed out. The farmer picked it up, just a plain old smoked glass bottle. He looked it over and started to laugh, and laughed so hard he started to cry. Personally, I thought that was overdoing Wayne's plight a bit. It turned out, though, that the farmer was not laughing at Wayne, but at something else entirely.

"That old so and so!" "It really was true after all!", he repeated over and over. Gradually, he got control of himself, and between gales of laughter, he dried his eyes and told us his story.

It seemed that his bachelor uncle had lived on that farm, with his old maid sister, for many years. They had died within months of each other, some 3 or 4 years before. The family was surprised and perplexed when it

31

was learned that the old man had amassed a considerable estate, consisting of 4 farms, rental buildings in town, and sizeable cash accounts in banks in each of the surrounding towns.

One time, we were told, the Uncle and his sister had gone into the bank to close on a farm that they had purchased. They brought a cream can with them, and when the banker asked them how they wanted to pay for the farm the old man upended the cream can on the table and out poured stacks and stacks of bills. The banker was a little startled at the sight of so much cash, but gamefully counted it out into neat piles that nearly filled the table. When he was finished. he checked over the piles and announced to the couple that the final count was $38,500, some $6,000 less than the amount needed to complete the transaction.

"Well, that sure is strange", mused the Uncle. "I could have sworn that I counted that out right".

After both parties had counted a couple of more times, and agreed as to the amount, the Aunt got up out of her seat and walked over to the table, then picked up the cream can.

"Well, Will, don't you see? You got the wrong cream can!"

"I never could see how he accumulated all his money." said the farmer. I have farmed this farm since he died, and never did make any money off it. And yet every few years, from the end of the World War (I) till Roosevelt came into office, he'd buy another farm or a building or open up another bank account. They never spent any money on themselves, or anyone else. Yet, every few months he'd drive up to Canada to see an old

Aunt of his. It made no sense. He never was devoted to anybody".

"From time to time, when I was a kid growing up, I had heard rumors about my Uncle selling bootleg whiskey. He was such a churchgoing pious so and so, and my aunt was worse, that I dismissed the rumors". " And yet, when they died in the early 30's I did scour this farm looking for a still. When I couldn't find any signs of illegal booze, I was a little bit ashamed that I'd suspected him. And to think that you boys found what I had been looking for all these years."

"It's clear as a bell now, what he'd been doing." "All those times he went to Canada to see the old Aunt were just a cover for the real reason for the trips. He must have had a contact in Canada who supplied him with liquor all during the years of Prohibition. He'd drive up there, bring back the liquor, then transfer the cases out of the car and into the wood pile. People could come here to make their pick up. I wouldn't put it past the old buzzard to have used the church's parking lot as a pick up point on Sundays too." "If that doesn't beat all!"

The farmer was still chuckling to himself as he started to dismantle the ends of the woodpile to get a better look at the inside of the Uncle's remarkable storage shed. We packed up and took our leave, glad that his temper had changed, but still concerned that he might get upset again when he noticed that his upstair's window was broken out.

On the way back to town Wayne repeated over and over how he had thought all along that there was something fishy about that woodpile and suspected that there was probably some sort of illegal activity connected with it, and it was just a matter of time till he would have solved the mystery.

Finally, after hearing Wayne's explanation one too many times, Clint said, rather too forcefully, "You know, Wayne, you wouldn't know a mystery if you fell into it!"

The Star of Justice--Romaine

During the first quarter of this century Plainview was a regular stop for numerous traveling entertainment groups. Many of these groups traveled by rail, and the usual place for the entertainment to be held was at the Opera House, located on the upper level of the buildings on the north side of Locust Street, east of Melvin's Paint Store, all the way to the alley. Entrance was from the alley, up a long flight of stairs.

The Opera House was the cultural and social center in its day. Political debates were held there, as well as dances. And during the season there were numerous plays, both by local amateurs and traveling professional companies, given for the entertainment of the public. The name, Opera House, while perhaps a bit misleading, reflected the name that most entertainment centers carried in small towns of the day. But it did describe the hall to some extent, as traveling opera singers and small groups on several occasions performed on the Opera House stage.

The Opera House was also the home of the high school basketball teams, before the new high school, with its modern gymnasium, was built in 1920. Elmer Pond and Harry Drake both played basketball at the Opera House, and reported that the facility worked quite well, except that the ceiling was so low that one was not able to get much arch on his shot. Since there were no showers or dressing rooms at the Opera House the boys were required to don their skimpy uniforms at the pool hall, in the south part of the bank building, then dash across the intersection and up all those steps, sometimes in the snow.

As the new school gymnasium served more and more as the home of many of the community functions, the public use of the Opera House was phased out, and then, for many years, until the new Masonic Temple was built in 1958, the Opera House was used as the Meeting Hall for the International Order of Odd Fellows, as well as the Temple for the Masons and Eastern Star members.

Perhaps inspired by the popularity of the Chautauqua Tent shows out of New York, which swept the country with their culturally uplifting programs, Plainview was regularly host to numerous tent shows over the years, until supplanted by the superior talent offered by movies and radio.

Still, well into the 30's, Plainview was served by a number of these attractions, held in tents. Each summer we were visited by traveling evangelists, who stayed for several days and served up an ample dose of fire and brimstone, old fashioned, gospel preaching. These revivals were well attended, and for some weeks afterwards there would be a marked increase in attendance at the local churches.

One time we had a promoter who brought a full sized whale, well preserved in formaldehyde, to town in a specially constructed semi-truck. There were long lines of people who paid to see this unusual, if smelly, attraction.

Before the war we also had a band of gypsies who regularly traveled through Plainview, and set up their camp in Dufek's grove north and west of town. While they were in the vicinity, the gypsy men would do odd jobs in town. One fellow's specialty was repairing holes in pots and pans. The women would tell fortunes. In the evenings, at their camp, they would perform spirited dances to the accompaniment of violins and tambourines. Afterward they would duly pass the hat for contributions. This part of their visit was fun. However, the arrival of the gypsies was also the signal for everyone to lock everything up, as there invariably would be a rash of thievery while they were in the vicinity, for which the gypsies got full blame.

Once, at least, in the 30's we had a Wax Museum which set up in a tent in a location downtown. There were a number of very life-like wax figures on display, including one section devoted to the famous criminals of history. That was scary, made more so by the fellow who lectured as he led the tour and described the grisly crimes that these people had committed. My sister, Judy, age 4, somehow got lost from our group. When we caught up with her she told how she had asked the "lady" where we were, but got no answer. The "lady", of course, was a very convincing wax usherette.

Of all the tent show companies that came through Plainview during my time, I believe that The Justice-Romaine Company was my favorite. This was a troupe of actors who set up their tent in the vacant lot on Locust Street, where the Mitch's Food Center Grocery now stands. They would be in town for most of a week, giving a different show each night. Their repertoire consisted of dramas, mysteries, comedies and variety shows. It was rumored that on Saturday night they would have a late show which was very risque, for adults only.

My folks limited me to just one of the Justice-Romaine Shows during the week, and I usually chose the comedy, in which Mr. Justice played the part of the country bumpkin, Toby, who invariably outwitted the city slickers in the third act. Between acts the actors would go up and down the aisles and hard sell boxes of chewy candy, with promises of cash and merchandise prizes in some the boxes. My folks thought that the candy was horribly overpriced, and was a needless extravagance, so I never did know how it tasted.

One week that the Justice-Romaine group was in town, however, I got to attend a second performance of the troupe, the variety show. That was because my friend and playmate, Mickie White, was going to perform in that show.

Mickie was a very pretty little girl. She had a constant smile and a pleasant personality. She also displayed considerable musical talent at an early age. She and I were the same age, at the time about 7 or 8. Since her folks had the cafe near the bakery, and we lived above the bakery, we were thrown together frequently, and we became great pals.

About this time in our life a young woman started a dance studio in Plainview, to teach the rudiments of ballet and tap dancing. Mickie was going to attend classes there, and I got my folks to send me as well. I'm sure that the young teacher was very good. The problem, for me, was that there were perhaps 20 or 30 little girls in the class, but only a couple of boys besides me. I'm sure that the influence of Shirley Temple, the best known child star of the day, had more influence on the girls than Fred Astaire did on the boys. With all those girls, the class suddenly was not as much fun, and I dropped out after just a few sessions.

Most of the people in the dancing class were very stiff, with two left feet, who clumsily tried to follow the simple steps. But Mickie White could actually do those

38

steps, and frequently demonstrated the steps for the rest of us. In no time she had mastered enough steps to really dance, and danced so well, in fact, that Mr. Justice asked her to appear on the troupe's variety show.

I'm sure that an 8 year old can not be a reliable critic, but for me that show was the best ever. Here was my friend, Mickie, singing, dancing, trading quips with Mr. Justice and the rest of the company, just as if she had been born into that setting. To me she was just as good as Shirley Temple in the movies. No, she was better! It wasn't just my opinion. The hometown audience gave her a thunderous ovation, proud as punch of our local celebrity, the Star of Justice-Romaine.

ACTIVITIES IN PLAINVIEW

The Skating Pond

It must have been late in the fall of 1941, just before the start of World War II, and we were in Mrs. Chase's 8th grade government class. The subject concerned ways in which individual citizens could affect the workings of government and make themselves heard. One of the ways discussed was the petition. Mrs. Chase was always on the lookout for practical ways to demonstrate a point, and when someone mentioned that we needed a place to skate in Plainview and that we ought to petition the city council to construct a skating pond, she immediately took up the point. She helped us draft the petition, then arranged for members of the class to take copies of our proposal to each class in the grade and high school, explain our proposal and ask for their help.

By the end of the second day we had an impressive stack of petitions, signed by almost every student and teacher. I remember that I, along with one or two others, was designated to deliver the petitions to Elmer Pond, probably because he lived in our neighborhood. Elmer was a hometown boy who had attended the University of Nebraska, then went off to Mexico and other places to drill for oil, and after a few years of prospecting in out of the way places of the world, came home to run for office. At this time he was the Pierce County Commissioner for the district that included the City of Plainview.

Never has a group of concerned citizens gotten faster action from a submitted proposal. Elmer thanked us for our interest and said he would see what he could do. The next afternoon I was downtown when Rusty Sterner, who operated the city road maintainer, stopped me. "I hear you kids want a skating pond. I'm ready to start the dirt work tomorrow morning." I was overjoyed. That petition was really a powerful tool for getting things done. It was only later that we learned that the city fathers had planned all along to construct the skating pond. Our petitions had just happened to come along after the fact. But they were kind enough to let us think that we had influenced their decision.

True to his word, within a few days Rusty and the other city workers threw up a shallow earthen breastwork perhaps ten yards outside the perimeter of the football field (which at that time was located just north of the present grade school building in Bandshell Park). Then, though it seemed like a very long time to us, it was probably only a few weeks until the weather turned cold and they were able to flood the pond. For this part of the process the men hooked up large fire hoses to hydrants at either end of the pond, and let the water run all during the night.

Here we were extremely fortunate, because during this time there was no snow and very little wind, so that the water going into the pond froze into a very smooth surface. We also received a bonus. Through some mix up in communication the water was not turned off when the water in the pond had sufficient depth, and for almost 48 hours over the weekend water filled the pond, and then continued to flow over a low spot in the levee and flooded most of the remaining surface of the entire park. The result was a huge frozen lake.

The weather for the next weeks remained ideal for skating, cold, but with very little snow. Skating became a very popular pastime, after school, and in the evenings. Granted, most of the skaters were young people, but

42

there was a representation of adults as well, all eager to test their skills on the ice.

Skates became a popular item, and the stores quickly sold out. In 1941 there were very few skates with the boots attached. Most were the clamp on variety, which used a key or clamp to fasten the skates to the soles of the shoe. Attics and basements were raided in hopes that antique skates, long discarded, might be salvaged for one more season's use.

The Winter Olympics on television, which has made figure skating so very popular, was still decades away, but Sonja Henie, the darling of the 1936 Olympics had made a few movies, so we were familiar with the rudiments of figure skating and tried to do the simple figure 8's with grace. One girl had a beautiful pair of white top figure skates, of which she was justly proud. The problem was that they were size 10 and simply did not offer the support that her size 6 feet and ankles needed, so her skating consisted mostly of moving around the pond slowly, on the inside of her ankles.

My Dad had picked up a pair of shoe skates for me at a farm sale. They fit me pretty well, but they were racing skates, with the blades that stuck out some 4 inches in front. They didn't make me an especially fast racer, but they did expose me to a great deal of ridicule, as no one had ever seen such skates before.

Ice hockey that winter was popular. In all of Plainview there was but one hockey stick, but everyone seemed to be able to come up with a tree branch with the general shape that worked quite as well. Of course there were no hockey pucks to be had, but after a bit of experimenting with stones of varying shapes we settled on a tuna fish can that worked perfectly fine. After the

43

holiday Bill Foft was the envy of the entire neighborhood when he arrived at the pond with his Christmas present, a pair of real hockey skates, complete with the rigid toe.

Pump pump pullaway was a popular game in which large numbers of skaters participated. This was a type of tag in which everyone lined up on one side of the pond, then tried to escape to the other side past one person, in the middle, who was "It". Those caught would in turn try to capture others, this going on until all were captured, whien the game would begin again.

Crack the Whip was fun. In that a line of people would join hands, the bigger boys in the lead, then skate around the pond until a considerable momentum was reached. Then the leader would pull the line into a tight turn which, by centrifugal force, would cause the last in line to go flying across the ice at great speed, very often out of control.

Some of the older boys started to show off a bit by jumping over barrels placed on the ice. Some of the leaps were quite spectacular, clearing some 5 barrels (and boxes). It should be added that some of the crashes were every bit as spectacular.

In the evenings there was often a large bonfire. People brought kindling and logs and tires to burn. Several times a group of us brought wieners and marshmallows to roast and we had a regular party. There were no portable radios, of course, but once a boy parked his car close to the fire and turned up his radio to the dance tunes of the day, so that time, at least, we had a big band accompanying our singing.

With the additional flooding there was plently of room for everyone. Those engaged in the active games might occupy the main portion of the pond, but there was still ample space for couples to skate, by the light of the moon, arm in arm, all over the park, around the trees and fountain, almost to the steps of our house across the street to the west.

The skating pond was truly a successful project. It brought a bit of pleasure to our town in that dark, sad, first winter of WWII.

THE PLAINVIEW KLOWN BAND

In July, 1995, I was invited back to Plainview to be the Master of Ceremonies at a program honoring the Plainview Klown Band on the 40th anniversary of their founding.

In 1955, to call attention to Klown Daze, a celebration which the Chamber of Commerce was planning, the town fathers asked Foy George to form a band that would travel to surrounding communities, drum up interest in the upcoming festivities, and bring more people to Plainview.

This was a natural for Mr. George, to form his fourth band in the Plainview area. In 1922 he had been hired by a few leaders in the Eden Valley Community, northeast of Plainview, to organize their musicians into a band, to give their young people something constructive to do. Soon after that he was asked to do the same thing in Plainview.

For two years he was paid entirely from donations contributed by the Eden Valley farmers and the Plainview business men. This changed in 1924 when he introduced a band music program into the Plainview Schools system. Since Mr. George did not have a music degree it was considered awkward for the school to hire him as a band director. So the community introduced a special band tax levy to pay Mr. George's salary, and that form of payment lasted for the next 40 years, until Mr. George retired from the Plainview Schools.

Members of the Plainview Town band formed the nucleus of the original Klown Band in 1955. The Town Band, made up of school bandsmen and interested bandsmen of all ages, met for practice on Monday nights for many years. Performances of the Town Band were rare during the school year, but during the summers the Town Band played a concert each Friday night. These concerts were originally held in the large gazebo in Chilvers Park. After 1938, when the new bandshell was built, as a WPA project, the concerts were moved to the park, on north Main Street.

The only charter member of both the Plainview Town Band and the Klown Band, besides Mr. George, was Joe Ruzicka. In the early days, Dr. Joe, a dentist, played the trumpet in the Town Band and served as assistant director. But later, during the time I played in the Town Band, and during his tenure with the Klown Band, he played the big bass tuba. Joe was a showman, and loved to perform, while Foy George was quiet and retiring, and shunned the spotlight. So Joe Ruzicka always announced the musical pieces that the band was going to play, in the early days with a large megaphone, and later with an electronic loud speaker system. But Mr. George knew what pleased a crowd, and early on he frequently featured Joe, barely 125 pounds, with his big bass tuba, with Wilfred Hughes, a rural mail carrier, in excess of 300 pounds, with his piccolo, playing solo parts in Sousa's "Stars and Stripes Forever". This Mutt and Jeff combination invariably brought down the house. But they played good music and were a credit to the band, as well as providing a good bit of comedy at the concerts.

In the 50's the Klown Band was used primarily to promote Klown Daze in surrounding towns. They typically would head south to Newman Grove or Tilden, play a short concert on the main square, then give a little spiel about the Klown Daze while a crew put up advertising flyers in the stores and bars; then proceed to the next town to repeat the process. During the booster trip they might hit 10 or 15 towns before returning to Plainview. Initially the band dressed up in Klown Kostumes, and Mabel Trump supervised making up each member's face in the prescribed Klown manner. It was immediately noted that the make-up made it difficult to play the instruments, and the make-up was hopelessly smeared after the first number. After that, only the director (after 1958, Louie Petersen) appeared in full make-up; the band members wore Klown Kostumes, but no make-up. A story about Director Petersen--Louie and his wife sometimes get into spats, but they always kiss and make up--Louie gets the Kiss and his wife gets the Make-up.

Jackie Bomar was a member of the Klown Band in the 50's. He says that some of those early members took their flyer distribution work very seriously. They thought that it was not right to ask to put up a poster in a bar without buying something, but after the 3rd or 4th bar they would sometimes forget to leave their posters, and after a few towns they would decide that they might just stay in the car and nap instead of playing the concert. Stories got back to Plainview about how good a time some of the members were having, and some of the citizens did not feel that they were projecting the right image for the town.

Marie Story, a teacher in the school, and Plainview's answer to Carrie Nation, was the leading advocate of a non-drinking policy for the Klown Band. She took it upon herself to see to it that the band remained sober on these booster trips, and volunteered to go along and ride herd on the Klowns on their next trip.

Les (Sticker) Thomas, a trombone player, seemed to be the member who required the most attention, so she stayed very close to him. (It might be pointed out that Les Thomas had gotten his introduction to the trombone by playing for church in his native Iowa.) Marie thought that she had been entirely successful in keeping Les on the straight and narrow, but when they got to Neligh, the third town on the tour, Les did seem to be having a grand time. Trouble was detected on the band's first number. Les was playing, but he sounded terrible. Stub Couchman, also a trombone player, glanced over and noted that while the announced number was on page #14, Les was playing on page #19. But he was playing with so much enthusiasm that no one had the heart to correct him. Marie was heard to explain, "I stuck to him like glue. The only time I left him was when he went to the bathroom. The man's impossible!" She gave up keeping the band straight after that.

Over these 40 years there have been some 70 members of the Klown Band, but as of 1995, the only charter member of the group is Stub Couchman, who started playing his trombone in Mr. George's band in 1930. When you consider that the band plays some 20 engagements a year, that figures to be some 800 Klown Band occasions. 800 times that Stub could have been working in his yard, or painting his house, or maybe taking a nap. He has surely enjoyed his association with the group, and enjoys playing with the band. But a man with dedication to the group like Stub has must have an understanding wife, and Stub does. In addition, Stub's wife, Lorene, has had the responsiblity of keeping the scrapbook on the Klown Band for its 40 year existance. It was a distinct pleasure for me to present a plaque from the Chamber of Commerce, along with congratulations and thanks from the community, to Stub and Lorene, who accepted on behalf of the Klown Band.

Stub, along with all the members of the band have had to endure their share of kidding over the years. The story goes that one time the band was playing at a celebration at Verdigre. One elderly farmer came from out of the hills to see the show. He recognized most of the instruments in the band, but was not familiar with the slide trombone. He was fascinated, and watched Stub for a long time. Finally he turned to his wife and said, "Ma, there's got to be a a trick to it. He's not really swallowing that thing, is he?"

At the 1995 ceremony the current members of the Klown Band were also inducted, as Admirals, into the Nebraska Navy by former band member, Leonald Warneke, on behalf of Governor Nelson. Governor Nelson also sent a letter of congratulations and thanks to the band for the goodwill the band has generated over the years. In his letter the Governor called attention to the band's record of 37 years of performing at the Nebraska State Fair.

Whenever you visit with someone about the Klown Band you pretty soon hear a story about the Klown Band Bus. Louie Petersen, in addition to his role as the band's director and figurehead, is the chief mechanic, and has kept the bus going for many years. It is always the same story. Just fix it up, and keep it going for another year. Over the years the bus has broken down on more than one occasion. Once they stalled on the viaduct just south of Norfolk and had to push the bus off the viaduct, and to the side of the road while they waited for other transportation.

One time the band was staying at a motel in Lincoln. They were scheduled to perform at the State Fair, but the traffic on the street in front of the motel was so heavy that they were unable to leave the motel parking lot. Mel Dierks decided that he could handle the situation. In his Keystone Kop Kostume he ventured out onto the street, blowing his whistle and holding up his hand, he stopped the traffic. He motioned to the bus to proceed, and then calmly stepped aboard the bus. There were no further delays and the band made it to the Fair on time.

Louie Petersen has made a practice of giving out suckers to children who attend the band's appearances at the State Fair. Over the years Louie estimates that he has given out more than 40,000 suckers, just at the Fair. He gives these suckers out with a flourish, an exaggerated gesture in which his little finger is extended, much as a society matron accepting a cup of tea at a snooty tea party. Parents, even grandparents, are now herding their youngsters toward the band at the State Fair to receive a sucker from the Chief Klown even as they had done as a child.

In 1963 the Omaha World Herald featured a picture of the Klown Band on the cover of their Magazine of the Midlands section, with a feature story by James Denney. The band immediately became quite famous throughout the area. When Grit Magazine, with a circulation of one million carried the story in June, 1964, the band was swamped with invitations to play at celebrations all over the country.

In 1979 the Klown Band was presented the Distinguished Service Award by the Plainview Chamber of Commerce, recognizing their work as good will ambassadors over the years. In July, 1984, at the Plainview Appreciation Day Celebration, the band was presented the Ak-Sar-Ben Good Neighbor Award.

It was particularly appropriate, I felt, that the Ceremony honoring the Plainview Klown Band for their 40 years of serving the community was held, on Friday night, at the Band Shell, the site of so many many Friday night band concerts over the years. It was a thrill for me to listen to a concert, there, in that park, across the street from the home where I grew up.

Listening to the Klown Band's happy polka music, it was easy to go back 40 years and more, to conjure up the memory of Mr. George, directing the band with his right hand, while playing his own trumpet (fingering the instrument with his left hand). And Joe Ruzicka tapping on his microphone, then blowing into it repeatedly to be sure it was on, getting ready to announce the next number. And Raymond Miller, getting everyone in a dance mood with his solo part in the "Clarinet Polka". Bob Couchman was a crowd pleaser with his solos in "Lassus Trombone", and "Hold That Tiger". And Curt Weatherhogg, soaring into the stratosphere on those high trumpet parts. And all of the guys and gals who played in the band with me, some really outstanding musicians, some, I'm afraid, pretty ordinary. But no matter. We had fun in the band. I'm grateful for the experience. And I'm very grateful that the Plainview Klown Band continues to keep alive the tradition of fine band music in Plainview. They are certainly deserving of all the accolades which continue to come their way. May they continue their merry musical ways for many many years to come.

52

The Plainview Chess Club

In the years leading up to World War II, Plainview was blessed with numerous organizations, both the organized variety, such as The American Legion, The Eastern Star, The Women's Club, and the various church organizations, but also the informal variety, such as the few friends that got together on a more or less regular basis to enjoy a common interest, like the various card clubs, the reading club that met at the library, and one of the strangest, from my viewpoint as a child, The Chess Club.

Chess was quite a popular game in the 30's. It's popularity, I believe, tells a great deal about the pace of life in the 30's. Of course, no one had any money. People did not travel, and they did not entertain lavishly. Chess did not cost money to play, and it took a lot of time, which people seemed to have more of in those days.

My folks played chess often in the evening after they got my sister and me off to bed. My Dad regularly slipped away from the bakery in the afternoon. Often he took a nap, since he worked the early hours of the morning, but frequently he could be found, if absolutely necessary, at one of his favorite haunts; the doctor's office next door to the bakery, with Dr. L.A. Johnson; at the depot, with stationmaster, Al J. Foster; or most frequently at the lumber yard with manager, Jack Pubanz, for an hour or so of chess. It still seems incredible to me that industry could stop for that period of time, but it happened.

Jack Pubanz, especially, was very fond of chess. He had become a devotee of the game while serving aboard ship in the Navy during World War I. If something would interupt the game at the lumber yard, he would put the chess board up on his file, to be resumed another day. He had one friend, who lived in the country, with whom he carried on a long distance game of chess. Each morning, when the friend's teenager would come to town for school he would bring a cryptic note to the lumber yard, spelling out a chess move, ie: Rook to Queen 7. Jack would go to a chess board which he kept set up for that game, and make the move. After school, the boy would again stop at the lumber yard to pick up the note spelling out Jack's move, to take home to his father. The game might go on for weeks.

The period of time I refer to now must have been in the middle 30's. We had moved to the house across from the park, but had not been there very long. Once a month, or it could have been oftener, the Plainview Chess Club would meet at one of the member's houses for an evening of chess, and supposedly, fellowship. There must have been eight members in the club, because there would be four tables set up in the house.

On the night that the Chess Club met at our house, I would be both pleased and sad. Dad liked oyster stew, and usually served that to the Chess Club. I loved oyster stew, so my mother always managed to prepare enough extra for me. That was good. But Chess Club meant that I had to stay out of the living room during the entire evening. This was difficult, because the only radio of the house, a Zenith Console, was in the living room, where the chess tables were set up. That meant that my sister and I had to stay in the kitchen or go to

54

bed. Sometimes we played a game, or my mother read to us. But we had to keep still.

It was a very strange sensation when the chess games started. Where there had been the usual banter of men when members arrived, once time started for a game, there was absolute silence, that would last for most of the 30 minutes or whatever the time limit was. It was like a tomb, and we whispered in the kitchen. Toward the end of the time limit you could hear, in subdued tones, "Check", meaning the opponent's Queen was in danger of capture, which would be the end of the game. And finally, "Checkmate", meaning that there was no longer any move that would prevent the capture of the Queen. "Checkmate" would signal the futility of further play and would be answered with "I resign", and the game would be over. When the little buzzer would go off all play would cease, and any unfinished games would be declared a draw. Then you would hear conversation for a few minutes, mostly congratulations to each other about how they had played the game, until the next game started.

Always at least once in the evening there would be raised voices,

"I didn't mean to move there."

"You took your hand off your piece!"

"No, I didn't, it just slipped out of my hand."

That would be Martin Sorensen, the postmaster. He seemed to use a feint with his chess piece as part of his strategy to determine what his opponent was going to do.

At 9 p.m., lunch was served, and then there would be one more game, and everyone would go home. For this last game, players would keep their coffee cups, or glasses of beer at the table with them and sip throughout the game.

Apparently we did not keep beer in the house in those days, and my sister, only three or four at the time, was not familiar with what it was. The morning after one of these chess parties, she got up early and went into the living room to inspect the aftermath of the party. At a couple of the tables there were small amounts of the beer left in the glasses. She took one sniff of the vile liquid, turned up her nose, and promptly dumped the contents into the toilet.

Jack Pubanz must have been the heart of the Chess Club because when he was transferred to the company headquarters in Minneapolis the Club quietly died for lack of a leader. Also, a number of the members of that Club were older men and some of them died or retired. Then too, as the 30's wore on, the pace of life quickened. In my dad's case, he gained some younger friends.

Dean Allen came to Plainview to manage the J.C. Penney store, and Dr. M.A. Johnson took over Dr. L.A. Johnson's practice. These two fellows were fun loving, and a lot more active than the average member of the Chess Club. The result was that we got a ping pong table in our basement and the Ping Pong Parties that replaced the Chess Club were definitely more to my liking.

THE INSTITUTION
THAT WAS SATURDAY NIGHT

In the days before World War II Saturdays were different in small towns in the midwest. To say that they were bigger and of more importance in people's lives that Saturdays are today is an understatement. They were an "Event" that people looked forward to with anticipation, not unlike the feeling we have now on the day before Thanksgiving or Christmas.

Plainvew, Nebraska, pop.1411, was what you would call a one-industry town. That industry was farming. Everything revolved around the farmer. The farmer dictated store hours and everything else in Plainview. And why not! Without the farmers' business there was no reason to exist. But the street ran both ways. Farmers were catered to in the extreme; merchants tried their best to serve the farmers with goods and services, and the farmers traded "at home".

My folks, Walter and Lenita Sehnert, had the bakery in Plainview when I was growing up. Saturday was the biggest day of the week. The bakery did as much business on Saturday as during all the rest of the week. The bakers would start as early as 9 p.m. on Friday, and would try to be finished with the baking by 1 or 2 p.m. on Saturday, all one shift. The store would open for retail business beginning about 7 a.m. on Saturday, and with luck, customers would have picked up their orders by midnight. Only then would the salesgirls be able to lock up and go home. But then all businesses did the bulk of their trade on Saturday. The only difference was that the bakery had to bake their product fresh each day.

Activity would' begin early on Saturday morning. Stores would be busy, but most of the activity would be in preparation, for the selling would not begin in earnest until after noon. Farmers would begin arriving early in the afternoon, though some of the richer farmers, who could use the excuse of having to come to town early, for repairs or a special sale at the sale barn, could be found having dinner at one of the two cafes on Locust Street.

First stop for a farm family was usually at one of the cream and egg stations. The five- and ten-gallon cream cans and the 30-dozen cases of eggs were hauled in the trunk of the family car. the check for the cream and eggs were an important part of the money that the family had to spend. The grocery stores also bought eggs and used the price they paid for eggs as an enticement for the farmer's wife to buy her groceries at that store.

There were six grocery stores in Plainview, all in the two blocks of Locust Street, the main commercial street. People would stop at the grocery store soon after they arrived in town and leave their grocery list. This list would be filled by grocery clerks who put the groceries into boxes, then placed them on the floor in front of the shelves. It was not unusual to go into a grocery store in the evening and find the walls completely lined with boxes of groceries waiting to be picked up. This might not happen until after the second show at the theater, but time didn't matter. Like the bakery, grocery stores could not close until the groceries were picked up.

One time this caused a sticky legal problem for Howard and Evie Craven, who operated the Food Center Grocery. For a period of several weeks, occasional boxes of groceries, that had been left at the store, were missing when the customer returned. Eventually the Cravens apprehended the culprit and started legal proceedings against him. Mrs. Craven was chagrined when the County Judge threw the case out of court and lectured her, saying, "Evie, those groceries were sold to other people, so no longer belonged to your store. You have no basis to sue anyone." Of course the wronged customer did not see it that way. He refused to bring charges, so the whole affair was dropped.

The pool hall in Plainview was an unusual place. It served soft drinks, ice cream, and frozen candy bars, but no beer or hard liquor was sold and none was allowed to be brought in. This lack of spirits supposedly made Plainview's pool hall a more "gentle place", and mothers would be more likely to allow their young sons free access. And SONS it was, because the pool hall was strictly MALE territory. If a wife wanted a word with her husband, who was at the pool hall, she would come to the front door and ask that someone call him. He would then come to the front and they would talk at the doorway. There were NO lady pool players.

The owner of Plainview's pool hall was Homer Haskins, and Homer took his reponsibility as "Keeper of the Morals" seriously. Not only did he keep all forms of liquor out of his place, but he could be very firm in reprimanding a young pool player to cool his language over a missed shot, and on numerous occasions he invited one or several players to leave when the language or horseplay go a bit out of hand.

None of this seemed to diminish the popularity of the pool hall. While there was some activity at the pool hall every day, on Saturday night the place was packed. Not only was every table occupied, but all of the high chairs lining the walls on either side of the room were filled with spectators, or more probably, pool players waiting for a table. Even though beer and liquor were taboo, smoking was tolerated, and was very popular. On Saturday night a person could not see from the front of the building to the back because of the thick haze of cigarette and cigar smoke; indeed at times to was hard to see from one end of the table to the other, when lining up a difficult shot. It didn't seem to bother Homer, however. He had a built-in radar. Sometimes some of the younger players tried to respot the "8 ball" on the sly and play a little longer on their nickle, but it seemed that the minute that black ball dropped into the pocket Homer would miraculously appear to re-rack the balls and collect for another game.

Homer had another talent. He loved to swim in the lake at the Country Club, and could frequently be found there in the summertime. He had a large stomach, and wore an old fashioned bathing suit, with straps over the shoulders. Floating on his back was his specialty, and he would float for an hour or more at a time, with his glasses on, smoking a cigar, and reading a newspaper, his green eyeshade (from the pool hall) keeping the sun out of his eyes. Sometimes he would float too close to the diving platform and boys would do a "cannonball dive" into the water, trying to splash him enough to put out his cigar. But again, his built-in radar saved him, and he generally stayed out of range.

Saturday night was a night to see people, and the place to see them was downtown. By sitting in one spot on Locust Street, sooner or later a person would see everyone who was in town, since all traffic moved through that two blocks of the main business area. Because parking space was limited, it was imperative to arrive early to be assured a choice parking spot. One family, who had retired from the farm, and now lived in town, would regularly park their car in front of Fischer's Market at 5 p.m., go home for supper, then return at 7, to sit in the car and be on hand for people to stop and talk during the evening. This was a very good location, since it was next to the theater, and a good many people would stop to visit as they entered and left the show.

Teenage girls tended to practice the 30's version of cruising. They would walk up one side of Locust, cross over, and walk down the other side, repeatedly throughout the night. Usually they would be in twos and threes, arm in arm. Each time they met a similar group going the other way they would stop to chat for a moment. These groups would invariably be followed by a like number of boys trying to make conversation. The girls pretended

61

not to notice. These girls were always well scrubbed, and smelled of soap and freshly ironed dresses. For some reason, many wore their hair in curlers. Evidently, as important as Saturday night was, as a social event, it was more important that one's hair be fixed properly for church on Sunday.

Baby carriages and strollers were numerous on "The Street" as young mothers promenaded, showing off their new babies and toddlers, exchanging bits of gossip and childrearing tips with friends as they met. As these babies tired and fell asleep they would be taken to the car or to one of the stores, where friendly clerks would watch after the little ones while their mothers did a bit of shopping.

The sidewalk also became the playground of somewhat older boys and girls who engaged in various forms of tag while their mothers continued conversation which had begun inside the stores. These bigger children added further hazards to the smooth flow of traffic, as they darted in and out among the walkers.

In the '30's Plainview's businesses were specialized. Shoppers bought their groceries at the grocery store, but bought their meat at the meat market, and their bread at the bakery. The drug stores had soda fountains, but did not serve coffee. The beer halls served beer, but had no pool table. In line with this thinking, the theater showed movies, but did not sell popcorn. That service was provided by a great old gentleman whom we called "Popcorn Petersen". He had a gas-fired popper on a little cart which he pushed from his home in the eastern part of town. He parked outside the theater, fired up his popper, and from that location made popcorn for passersby and theater patrons throughout the night. That had to be the finest popcorn ever made, because like Orville Redenbacher of a later time, every kernel popped, and if one asked politely, Mr. Petersen would put on an extra shot of melted "real" butter, which soaked through the sack and made the hands greasy, but made that popcorn truly delicious!

The bakery was a few doors down from the theater. To take advantage of the Saturday night traffic, my Dad, Walter, bought one of the first automatic donut makers and installed it in the bakery show window. It was a grand "white enamel on steel" machine which stood about 5 feet high, and 2 1/2 feet on the side, with glass windows for viewing the donut-making process. The raw donuts dropped from a pressurized tank into the hot grease at 7 second intervals. They were floated in a circular path around the inside of the machine. Halfway around the course they were flipped over; then at the end of the circle the finished donuts were flipped again, down a chute into a wire basket where they could be stacked, awaiting sale or further processing. The complete cycle took two minutes, and the machine could turn out about 30 dozen donuts per hour.

The donut maker required a lot of adjustment and was a beast to clean, but the sight of all that synchronized dropping, flipping, and moving had a hypnotic effect on passersby, and when combined with the exhaust fumes, which were piped out onto the street, made those succulent little cakes darn near irresistible. Walter was sure that he had found the source of the expression, "Selling like Hotcakes".

Occasionally, there would be a band concert on Saturday night. This did not happen every week, but sometimes in summer, Mr. George would march his band up town to play a few numbers in the intersection by the bank. These mini-concerts were not as extensive as the Friday night concerts, but they did draw good crowds, and people would honk their car horns in appreciation after each number. The music served to get the evening's festivities off to a good start.

The theater did good business on Saturday night. There were always two shows, with cartoon, news reel, plus coming attraction, so the second show was not out until midnight or after.

It was Walter's custom to attend the movies on Saturday night. After working all Friday night and most of Saturday he was exhausted by show time, but he had to be somewhere until it was time to close the bakery, so he chose to go to the movies. He invariably fell asleep somewhere during the first reel and missed out on the rest of the picture. He was self-conscious about falling asleep during the movies and hoped that no one noticed. But one time a woman tried to talk the theater owners' wife out of buying a ticket for her good-sized youngster, saying the boy would just sleep through the show. Mrs. Hoffman's reply, in Walter's hearing, was, "Walter Sehnert has been sleeping through the movies every Saturday night for years and he never once asked to be admitted free!"

64

The library, in the middle of a friendly green expanse just one block north of the business district, was a popular place on Saturday. Many farm families made the library one of their first stops, to return the books that had been picked up the week before. It was not uncommon for a family to exchange 20 or more books and magazines. Remember, there was no TV, no paperback books, and magazine subscriptions were expensive, so many families took advantage of the library's liberal lending policy.

People could be found perusing books and magazines all Saturday evening at the library. The "people" were invariably women (with their children) who needed a place to wait for their husbands, who were at the tavern, or pool hall, or barber shop, or the filling station. But promptly at 9 p.m. all books had to be checked out because, unlike the bakery and the grocery stores, the library doors closed precisely at that hour.

The beer halls were busy, but they were off limits to teenagers. There was an exception, however. Baber's Cafe, on the main intersection, did serve beer, but their specialty was food, so minors were able to patronize that place freely. The cafe occupied two connecting buildings. One, on Locust and Main, had a long counter with stools, a few tables, a small bar, and a pinball machine. The second, just south on Main Street, had booths completely around a good-sized dance floor. On Sundays this was a very popular place for Sunday dinner, featuring fried chicken, homemade pies, and lots of homegrown vegetables, which were grown by

Gene Baber, as a hobby. But on Saturday night, the lights were low, the music loud, and the dance floor rocked. All the great bands were there, via their latest recording, on the juke box--Tommy Dorsey, Russ Morgan, Guy Lombardo and the rest. An entire generation of Plainview youths learned to dance to the strains of "South", "The One O'Clock Jump, "The Beer Barrel Polka", and "The Waltz You Saved For Me" at Baber's.

The "Institution That Was Saturday Night" was a phenomenon which was destined to end with the advent of good automobiles and good roads. Both of these were realities by the beginning of World War II, but the war caused everything to stay the same for another five or six years while we won the war and then recovered from its effects. Eventually, people were able to buy cars once more. Bridges were built, the roads paved, and hub towns assumed a more prominent role in people's lives. After the war people had more money. They had beautiful new cars and needed an excuse to use them. They did not have to come to town only once a week, they could drive to town every day, or choose a different town each day. So business was spread out more evenly over all the days of the week. Saturday became just another day.

The crowning blow to the "Institution That Was Saturday Night" was television. In the early '50's Saturday night had a good lineup of television fare, and television proved to be so alluring that people chose to stay home, rather than come to town on Saturday night. The magic of television brought new friends into the living room--Uncle Miltie, Sid

Caesar, Matt Dillon and Miss Kitty, among others. To a large extent, these new friends replaced the fellowship of talking to old friends and neighbors in person.

But so much for this trip down "Nostalgia Lane". I need to check on my grandchildren. They are very busy collecting impressions and experiences for an artice they will write, someday, entitled, "Life Back In The "90's".

AUTOMOBILES

Recently, while on a trip to Kansas City, I had the privilege of attending the 1995 Automobile Show at Bartles' Hall. It was truly an impressive event; the equivalent of eight football fields of new cars, representing the products of the world's auto producing elite (except the Yugo was not represented this year). I can only dream of the value of all the automobiles on display. It was as if a car nut had indulged his fancy after winning the super lottery. Each of the major manufacturers had a young woman in slinky evening dress describing their top of the line jewel of automotive genius, the girl and the car revolving slowly on a carpeted dais, beneath a spotlight to the accompaniment of soft music.

I'm sure that everything was designed to get the viewing public into a buying mood. I'm glad that I got to see it. I never was sure that I had even seen a Jaguar, or a Bentley in person. Now I know that I have. But rather than arousing lust in my heart for one of those beauties (cars), the whole show left me less bewitched, and more bothered and bewildered. For one thing, all of the engineers must have gone to the same school. The design for all of the cars was much the same, and I had trouble distinguishing the Toyota from the Cadillac, or the Chevrolet, or Chrysler, and on down the line.

Another thing. You used to be able to tell about how much you were going to pay by the make of car that you bought. No more. Now you can pay as much, or more, for a Chevrolet as you can for a Cadillac. And it is very hard to compare costs between brands. They have so many gradations within the product line, and so many package options that it is impossible to determine whether a certain Dodge car is a better deal than a certain Ford car. You very well could be comparing apples with oranges and not even know it.

Of course, the suggested retail price on these beauties could take your breath away. The fact that most of the cars cost more than we paid for our house tells more about when we bought our house than the relative value of houses and cars today, but still I found it a little amazing that one can still buy a rather substantial house for the money that they are asking for the upper end automobiles.

Plainview got into the business of selling automobiles in the early years of this century. The Hecht Implement Company, (later the Kuhl Implement Co.) owned by George and Charlie Hecht began selling Jackson Autos in 1907. In 1910 the featured entertainment for the Pierce County teachers who were attending an Institute in Plainview was an automobile tour of Plainview sponsored by the Scott Automobile Co. of Plainview (who did business in the building south of the public library), assisted by George Hecht, P.D. Correll, Fred Free, F.C. Holbert and their automobiles. It was reported that "The way they speeded around the square northeast of town made the schoolmarms hold their breath." About this time the city fathers took note of the proliferation of automobiles in the community and passed an ordinance which required drivers not to drive faster than eight miles per hours on the streets of Plainview. "All offenders will be prosecuted!"

The several livery barns that boarded horses and were in the business of renting buggies, wagons and horses were gradually replaced by auto dealers and filling stations. One of the most prominent livery barns, at the west end of Locust Street changed its business direction, and continues to the present time as Steinkraus Oil Co.

Though at one time or another most of the existing cars on the market were sold in Plainview, by the time that I have memory of automobiles we had but two dealers in Plainview. Otto "Dutch" Saathoff had the Chevrolet Garage (formerly Saathoff and Cline), in the building later occupied by the Headquarters cafe. And after many years as Ford dealers, the Kirks had sold out their agency and in the 30's and 40's it was known as Huey's Ford agency, in the building south of the Plainview National Bank building. Identifying and buying automobiles was quite simple because nearly everyone drove either a Ford or a Chevy, and in each brand one had but two choices, the Standard or the Deluxe model, plus a very limited choice of colors. There seemed to be a great loyalty in families to one brand or the other. School boys would argue incessantly over the merits of the two brands.

All during the 30's automobiles were purchased outright, with no financing available. Bill Ferguson told of making his living during those years as an automobile salesman in Plainview, during which time he never sold a car for more than $500, and never financed a car. Leo Steinkraus had an ongoing arrangement with the Hueys which allowed him to trade for a new Ford car each year for $100.

My folks came to Plainview in 1930, and were driving a Graham Paige, a large, beautiful car. Though my folks had bought it for very little money, they considered it to be pretentious in Plainview and soon

70

traded it off for a more modest Chevrolet. Thereafter, every other year, they would trade for a new Chevy. This went on until World War II, when because there were no civilian cars manufactured, their 1941 Chevy had to last until the war ended. After the war automobiles were extremely hard to get and dealers regularly accepted an additional payment "under the table" in addition to the government fixed price for a particular model. I remember so well how hurt my Dad was that Mr. Saathoff, from whom he had always bought his cars on a regular basis, felt compelled to ask for the "sweetener" from my Dad to buy a new Chevy. It caused a rift in their friendship which was never healed, and for the first time Dad went out of town to buy a car, a Packard.

After the war, Maurice White introduced the Chrysler product to Plainview. A great fanfare accompanied the first of White's new cars to town. Erhardt Hemmingsen had the distinction of being the first name on the list for that car, a dark blue, four door, Chrysler, which he was able to buy at list price. He immediately turned around and sold it to someone else for a substantial bonus, while he waited for the supply of cars to become more numerous, and cheaper.

Plainview had the distinction of having the first motorized hearse in the state of Nebraska, bought by P.F. Boyens, for the Boyens Mortuary (the building presently occupied by the Senior Center). This was really quite an anomaly, as I don't believe that Mr. Boyens ever was comfortable with an automobile. During the 30's one could always tell when P.F. was on the street, because he never shifted gears. If he started out in low gear from home that is the gear he kept for his entire trip, and his car could be identified, by the roar of the engine for blocks. This was probably a good thing as he didn't see too well either and people kept out of his way. The following story has been told about Mr. P.F. Boyens: He had just bought his first car, and had passed the demonstration test with the dealer. When he attempted to park the car in the barn at home, he got his feet mixed up between low gear and the brake and was was still pulling back on the steeing wheel crying "Whoa" as he crashed through the side of the barn.

Today if one drives near the high school he is struck by the number of late model cars parked there. If you had business with the school you would be forced to park at least a block away. In the 30's there were very few cars parked around the school, and those that were there were driven by farm boys, who ran their individual bus service for others in their neighborhood. No town kids drove to school, and very few faculty members did either. During the war years it was even worse, as gas and tires were rationed, and people were extremely careful to avoid unnecessary trips.

Since the use of automobiles was restricted, delivery jobs that involved a vehicle were in great demand. Pick-up trucks were not at all common, and light deliveries were made with cars for the most part. Houston's Grocery had a fairly large, early 30's truck with which Don Houston and Harold Mauck used to make the store's deliveries. Since it was quite a rarity for young fellows to have any vehicle to drive, these two made quite an impression as they made their rounds of delivering, demonstrating their driving prowess before an admiring audience of high school girls, and envious boys of all ages.

I have always liked the "old cars". Probably, trying to recapture some of the fun that we used to have in the

72

old Model T that Don DeMuth had in high school, several years ago I bought a Model T of my own, and have very much enjoyed driving it in parades and car rallies. We also have restored our wedding car, a 1951 Plymouth Belvedere, and consider it one of the family treasures. So do I consider myself a sentimentalist where old cars are concerned? Indeed I do! Would I like to go back to the days when cars were simpler, and cheaper? A few weeks ago, in February, wintertime no less, on a warm day, the air conditioner went out on our family car. Both my wife and I felt that we were terribly deprived, and could not wait to have the darn thing fixed. Those times are fun to reflect upon, but we find we like the new cars, with all the gadgets, expensive though they be. I like the here and now, with all its problems, and this is just where I want to be.

AN INTRODUCTION TO FOOTBALL

I couldn't believe how lucky I was. The year was 1942. The country was at war, but in Plainview it was fall and the start of another football season. For years I had loved the fall, and football season, and looked forward to its start all summer long. The younger guys, my friends below high school age, had always played in the Band Shell Park, next to the high school gridiron, and had watched the Pirates practice each night. After a time, a pick up game of football would get started. We would try to put into practice techniques that we picked up from the high schoolers. We pretended that we were playing for the Red and White, in front of cheering fans.

But that was just kids' stuff, and in the past. Now, here I was, at last, a full-fledged member of the Plainview High School football team.

"A full-fledged member of the team." That was not strictly true. I was a 105-pound member of the freshman class who had been allowed to come out for the team. They really didn't even have a uniform small enough for me. The pants of my first uniform were so long that the thigh pads banged against my knees. The next one was just a little better. But that didn't matter. As far as I was concerned, I was as much a part of the team as any of the lettermen. I just needed a chance to prove it.

I wasn't the only inexperienced presence on the field that fall. We also had a new coach. Don Button, who was married to Dutch Saathoff's older daughter, Happy, had come home from the service on a medical discharge, just in time to inherit the football coaching position at the high school. He really was not equipped, either from a knowledge or an experience standpoint, to be the head football coach, but this was wartime, and people filled in the best way they knew how, so he had agreed to take the job. One of his first acts, since he did not have a play book, was to buy a copy of "50 Basic Plays That Work" off the magazine stand at Bartlett's Drug Store. One of the other freshmen footballers told me that he was sure that it would be a successful season, because he had also bought one of those "50 Basic Plays" books at the drug store, and he thought that they really looked like great plays.

Coach Button was handed a rather nondescript team that first year. One of his jewels on that team, though, was Darrell Hamilton. Darrell was an upperclassman, a powerful fullback, and one of the largest men on the team. He was also one of the fastest, a really fine football player. He was also the cause of my not getting along very well with Coach Button. I thought that Coach Button was a man who did not keep his word.

Before the first game, an away game with Hartington, Coach Button told the scrubs, of whom I was a charter member, that we would have a scrimmage. In that scrimmage, if one of us freshmen could tackle Darrell, we would be added to the traveling squad for that game. On the play that was designated for our test, Ham broke through the line and eluded one, then another linebacker, and was headed for a sure touchdown. He had only one other defender to beat...ME! It was no secret that I was terrified. He must have outweighed me by 100 pounds, and could easily have gotten by me with a little dipsy doodle, or a stiff arm. For some reason, he chose to run right over me. When I saw that we were going to collide I closed my eyes and lowered my head and made a dive for his legs. I'm sure that it was the worst tackle that anyone ever made, but somehow it caused him to stumble, and after lurching forward for another ten yards, he fell to the ground.

I really don't remember if he scored on the next play or not. What I do remember, is that when the list for traveling squad was posted, I was not on it. When I reminded Coach Button of his promise, he scoffed, and said that mine was not a tackle, and that Darrell had just stumbled and fallen down. I pointed out that it was **my body** that had caused the stumble, but it was to no avail, and I missed traveling to that first game with the team.

Even though Coach Button was not my favorite person, I still could not have wished upon him the misfortune that befell his team and us that same week. We had finished the regular practice and had lined up at one end of the football field for a mass hundred-yard dash to the other end, where Coach would talk to us for a few minutes. I sought out Orville Foster, Earl's younger brother, for my special adversary. Orville was 15, a little older than I, but was much the same size, and he and I had been lining up beside each other, or against one another since fall practice had begun. He was a likeable kid, and we had hit it off immediately, comparing opinions about teachers, girls, and coaches. We had swapped a few stories and all in all had become friends, our common bond being the football team.

Orville accepted my challenge for the race, saying that he would be waiting for me at the goalposts. He said further, that I should try to hurry because he had to get home before dark. We both appreciated the good-natured banter, and went all out when the whistle blew to start the race. I don't remember who won the race. I think it was pretty close, run with the happy exuberance of youth. When we got to the finish line we were laughing as we plopped down on the ground to hear what the Coach had to say. We were still getting our breath when Orville, taking off his helmet, suddenly fell over on me. I thought that he was still goofing around, and pushed him away, only to have him collapse at my feet. I tried to turn him over, and noticed that he was turning blue. I'm sure that I panicked, and screamed for the Coach to come to help.

Coach Button grasped the situation immediately. He instructed one of the players to run to the school to call the doctor, and then proceeded to give Orville artificial respiration until Dr. M.A. Johnson arrived at the scene a few minutes later. Dr. Johnson injected something into Orville's arm, then pounded on his chest a few times, listening for a heartbeat each time. It wasn't long, though, before he got up and shook his head to Coach Button, and told him to send the team to the lockers. We all knew that Orville was gone.

It's strange, even after more than 50 years, when football season rolls around again, along with the fun of the game, the thrills, the expectations, and the disappointments that make up this season of the year, I think, too, of a fellow I only knew for a few days, but nevertheless was my friend. He never got to play the game of football or the game of life. But I'll always associate him with this time of year, and football.

THE COUNTRY CLUB

One of the things that made Plainview such a special place to live in the 1930's was the Country Club, located some five miles north and west of Plainview. This was a private facility, a fact that I was only vaguely aware of as a child. It was so much a part of my life. It was here that I learned to swim, to fish, to play golf. Summers, especially, seemed to be spent at the Country Club, with people that I knew. It was only later that I realized that the $25 per year dues made it a facility that was out of the price range for a great many people in the community. To the credit of the Country Club board of directors, the guest policy of the Club was lenient. The three visits per year rule for non-members was largely ignored, and non-member youths were encouraged to take part in the Red Cross swimming lessons, held at the Country Club.

The Country Club was a dream of a group of 30 civic leaders in 1924. Some of these men, with whom I was acquainted, were Drs. Fickling, Melerian, Cline, Jensen, and Nye; Lawyer John Blezek; Dairyman Les Hecht; Farmers Charlie Seabury and Chris Lerum; Telephone man C.W. Smith; Auto dealers Fred Weidman and George Kirk;, Harnessmakers Bob and Harry Johnson; Miller Tom McHenry; Insurance man Chet Christiansen; and Druggist Earl Odineal. These men bought 32 swampy acres from the Loftus farm and set out to build a dam and dredge out a recreational lake, entirely with volunteer labor.

Later they bought an additional 50 acres of sandy land across the road, with pledged and borrowed money for the golf course. By developing part of the new land into a gravel pit they were able to pay off all loans by 1936. By the time that I was aware the gravel pits were no longer active, but for years afterwards players were left with the most formidable sand trap that ever faced a golfer.

For some reason my memories of the Country Club are stirred by a sense of smell. For instance, as a child, as soon as the car door opened at the parking area above the swimming area, the smells that assaulted our nostrils, the lake water, the trees, the thick cover on the slope (grass, clover, plantain, and other short weeds that we now try to eradicate from our lawns). Running down the slope these scents all mingled together and added up to one giant sensation--Fun!

And run we did. It was always a race to see who could get to the bottom of the hill, and through the dressing rooms and into the water first. There was a low pier leading out into the lake some ten yards. Why we never did ourselves great bodily harm in running the length of that pier and diving into the lake I don't know. We were cautioned about diving too deeply from the end of the pier into the shallow water from an early age. In the early days of the Club some boyhood friend of Warren Hill had dived straight down from this pier and had broken his neck. Our parents used his experience as a warning each time we entered the water.

A little further out into the lake, perhaps 30 yards, there was a diving platform, with about an eight foot high diving board. To swim to the diving board was our goal from little on. Once you could swim that far you were considered an accomplished swimmer. There were benches all the way around the diving platform, and these were used extensively for sun bathing. I know that many a girl who regularly used the the diving platform for sunning, never did make the plunge from the board.

As I grew up in Plainview I began to assume another role, as far as the Country Club was concerned. I got my Red Cross Life Saving certificate, and eventually my Swimming Instructor's papers, and for a couple of summers assisted Lois Cline in the Water Safety program at the Country Club, and we taught a new crop of youngsters to swim. After a time I assumed Lois' position as head instructor, and my sister, Judy, became my assistant, and later, Judy took over the top position. It was always a thrill to see a fledgling swimmer make it to the diving board for the first time.

In the early years fishing was a very popular pastime at the lake. Bob and Harry Johnson had constructed a fish hatchery near the spillway of the dam and for years supplied the fish for the lake from that hatchery. Later the fish were stocked by the State Game Commission.

Early on the fathers of the Country Club built a boat house on the west edge of the lake, with a swinging bridge leading to it. Our family never did have a boat, but I loved that swinging bridge. It really did sway, and a favorite pastime was to get a couple of girls in the middle of the bridge and then to cause it to sway violently, just to listen to them scream. Later, when I was older, we used to swim under the doors of the boat house, unlock the doors from the inside, and "borrow" a boat for a leisurely ride on the lake.

Each year, to open the season, the Country Club would have an "Open Day", when families gathered to enjoy the facilities. Mr. George very often took the band

80

to play for this event. It was a popular outing, and people would come with picnic baskets, and there was a general holiday air, with impromptu softball games, horseshoes, and the most marvelous kids' playground facilities. The teeter-totters were extra long planks that gave a thrilling ride. The swings were high, and the seats were held in place by a series of 3 foot sections of iron rods instead of ropes. These swings brought you to the top of the trees it seemed. The sand box was huge, and lent itself to grand designs of roads, tunnels, and castles. These attractions were located just west of the club house, shaded by tall trees, and were very busy.

The Club House was completed in 1931. It was a large rough-finished building with a big fireplace on the west wall. On the east wall was a pump and a woodburning cook stove. The building, for sometime at least, was lighted by kerosene lamps in holders along the walls. There were a number of picnic tables through the center of the room, as well as more on the full length porch across the north side. Someone had shot an elk or large deer, and the head was mounted above the fireplace. It had been an impressive trophy, I'm sure, but eventually the mice got into the head and had eaten off the nose, and finally that treasure was reluctantly removed.

The Club House served as the meeting place not only for family picnics, but for the women's golf luncheons, and the men's golf stags. It also was the site of the annual Country Club meeting. I remember very well one such meeting---

Over the years various items had been donated to the Club House facility, fireplace andirons, salt and pepper shakers, pots and pans and the like. At this particular meeting a suggestion was made that the Club

81

House be locked, and each member given a key, as items had been reported missing. The pros and cons of the suggestion were talked about for awhile when one lady got up and said that she felt that such a step was unnecessary as she was sure that people just got things in their picnic baskets by mistake. At that point another woman got up and said, "Yes, and I suppose that the kitchen pump that came up missing last week was just put in someone's picnic basket by mistake too!" In the end it was decided that it would not be practical to lock up the building and it was hoped that the pump would not be stolen again.

Originally there had been a tennis court just east the the Club House, but it had been abandoned by my time in the middle 30's. The Country Club golf course proved to be the focal point of the entire organization from the beginning. In the 30's the golf course would have to be considered crude by today's standards. The fairways, watered only by nature's rain, were brown for most of the summer. The rough was tall and balls hit into that area were usually lost. The greens were sand, treated with waste motor oil, and there was a definite knack to smoothing the surface. Some golfers were skillful in fashioning a little trough that would bring the ball right into the hole. Until after WWII all maintenance was done with horse drawn (largely donated) equipment.

Still, the Plainview Country Club produced some very fine golfers. The Millnitz brothers come to mind as being among the best of the men golfers. Of the women, I shall mention but two, with whom I was well acquainted, Nell Fickling and Leone Logan Rowe. I caddied for these two in several tournaments and gloried in their triumphs, and agonized in their defeats. During this period men's and womens' golf tournaments at Plainview were well attended by golfers throughout the area, and Plainview enjoyed a fine reputation, not only for its fine facilities, but for its hospitality at these tournaments.

While most of my activity at the Country Club occurred during the summer, the facility was used throughout the year. In the winter there were a number of ice fishermen who found considerable success on the lake, even though that sport was considered dangerous due to the large number of springs in the lake which made the condition of the ice uncertain, and ruled out ice skating entirely.

The activity that I took part in at the Country Club in winter was that of sledding. Nell Fickling was very good about taking us to the Country Club in winter and pulling us, on our sleds, behind the car. It was great fun to speed around the fairways behind the car, and the mixture of exhaust fumes mingled with snow is a sensation I can feel to this day. Afterwards we would adjourn to the Club House, build a huge fire in the fireplace, and drink hot chocolate while we told tall stories and waited for our clothes to dry out.

It is with pleasure that when I go back to Plainview now that I see that the Country Club not only still exists, but that it thrives. The lake is not the hub for water sports that it once was, and air conditioning has caused the Club House to be superceded by the "10th Hole" as the meeting place of choice, but the swings and teeters are as popular with our grandchildren as they were with us, and the golf course rivals the best of the small courses in the state.

Selective Memories

This summer I attended the 50th reunion of the Plainview High School Class of '45. This was not the class with whom I had gone through school, but since we had been in school together for a number of years I had friends in the class and I had looked forward to seeing them all again.

It was not without a certain amount of apprehension that I attended their informal get together at the "10th Hole", a comfortable facility which was created west of the golf course, just off Country Club property (the Country Club constitution forbids alcohol on Country Club property, and that constitution apparently has never been changed.) The Class of '45 had taken their role of Upper Classmen seriously, and I wasn't sure just how I might be accepted 50 years later. I needn't have worried. Everyone was in a good mood, and there was none of the aloofness that perhaps I had imagined from 1945.

Fortunately, the "girls" in the class had thoughtfully provided name tags at the snack table, along with the potato chips and dip, which saved a good bit of embarrassment all around, as names were sometimes slow to come to mind. In no time at all the reserve that everyone had brought to the gathering was gone and laughter (with a few tears) filled the room as people and incidents from "way back then" were brought to mind. The "one-upsmanship" that was in evidence at earlier reunions, when people tried to impress their classmates with stories of fabulous jobs, great riches, big cars, and genius offspring, was nowhere to be seen. Everyone had

had their share of "life's little suprises" and we could laugh over a trivial incident of long ago even while we cried inside as we shared stories of illness, divorce, or death. There in that place we had all come home again and were genuinely pleased to be sharing a moment with old friends who "knew me when".

Leon Jensen, of the Class of '45, was sitting at a table, visiting with a small group and looking at some scrap books. I could see pictures of Leon with people like Hall of Famer, Ritchie Ashburn, and "Lefty" LaSorda, (now Tommy LaSorda, the LA Dodger Manager), who were both former teammates of his. Leon and I had played football and basketball together on the high school teams. Leon was perhaps the best athlete on the team, the quarterback on the football team, the shooting guard in basketball, and neither of these was even his best sport. He was also a fine baseball pitcher and had been a teammate of Ashburn's when the two had starred on the Neligh Legion Baseball team (Plainview had no Legion Baseball at that time). The two had gone into professional baseball together. Ritchie went on to baseball greatness while Leon ended his career early with a sore pitching arm. But that in no way diminished the high regard that I held for his athletic prowess then, and have held for all these years.

Thus it was that I deemed to go over to say hello and perhaps talk a little PHS football or basketball. As I approached the little group Leon looked up, gave me a big grin, and said, "Well here's the guy who caught the winning pass against Pierce!" Were it only so.

I knew exactly what he was talking about, and it was indeed my shining moment on the football field. Pierce, a perennially strong team in the conference, and

85

Plainview's arch rival, held less than a six point lead with about a minute to go in the game. We had mounted a drive which had seemed to fizzle out with 4th and 8 to go on about their 20 yard line. We had to pick up a first down, at the very least, or it was all over. In the huddle Leon called a pass play on which Kenny Hamilton, our star running back, was the primary receiver. I played right end and it was my job to drift across the middle and draw the linebacker to me, then when Kenny caught the ball to block someone. As so often happens in football, as in real life, things do not always happen as they are planned.

Evidently the Pierce team anticipated our play and Kenny Hamilton was hopelessly covered. Apparently everyone else was too, as I'm sure that I was the very last receiver to be considered, but that was the option that Leon took. At the last moment he fired a strike right at the numbers that I could not possibly miss. I could see the yard marker that I had to reach for the first down and put my head down and drove for that spot. Just as I reached the yard marker the Pierce linebacker hit me as hard as I've ever been hit in my life. I thought that he had broken me in half, but I held on to the football and we did pick up the first down. The drive was still alive.

I was sure that I was going to have to leave the game. I hurt all over and was just beginning to get up when I looked over at the fellow who had tackled me. He was lying on the ground beside me, out cold. The Pierce trainer and doctor were giving him smelling salts. When I saw that I suddenly didn't feel so bad and got up, a little gingerly, and limped back to the huddle. The whole team was patting me on the back and saying that we had the first down. Now we had a chance. The team was unanimous in saying, "We are going to win this game!" I felt like I'd just won the lottery. Oh yes, on the next play Kenny Hamilton took the ball on an off tackle dive, broke into the secondary and scored the touchdown. That touchdown really won the game.

I was in a dilemma. After 50 years, had Leon's memory faded a bit? Or did he have Selective Memory? Either way, I didn't correct him. No need to to embarass him. What if his version was the correct one? After all, it was just a game, 50 years in the past. But Gosh, he made me feel good!

PEOPLE IN PLAINVIEW

REMEMBERING FOY GEORGE

In Meredith Wilson's musical classic, "Music Man", Professor Harold Hill arrives in River City, and after working a bit of flim flam on the populace, saves the River City youth from "degradation" by organizing a band, earns the everlasting thanks of the town, marries the beautiful girl who sings like an angel, and everyone lives happily ever after.

In the early days following World War I, Plainview had its own "Music Man". Foy George came to town, formed not one, but three bands, married a beautiful girl who sang like an angel, and for 40 years taught us a little bit about making music, and a lot about making a life. In the process, without even a suggestion of flim flam, he earned the love and respect of the entire community.

Foy George was born in Ohio in 1896, but grew up in Carroll, Nebraska, and graduated from high school there in 1916. Already an accomplished musician, he enrolled that fall at Wayne State Normal School, a few miles down the road, to study music. Immediately, his unusual first name got him into trouble, when the registrar assumed Floy for Foy, and assigned him to the girls' dorm, strictly against the rules in 1916. That problem was soon rectified and he quickly adjusted to college life. He loved the school. He loved the course of study, and that year he played an important part in the brass section of the college band and orchestra.

However, 1917 found the United States at war, and Foy, like so many of his fellow students at Wayne, dropped out of school, enlisted in the army, and looked forward to serving in France. The army, however, recognized his musical talents, and after a short preliminary training, assigned him as an instructor in the band at Fort Sill, Oklahoma, where he served throughout the war.

Much later, during the Korean War, while I was stationed at Fort Sill, Mr. George wrote to me and described some of his experiences during his tour of duty there during World War I. Once, he said, the band, which was mounted on horses, was playing for a military funeral. He played taps at the conclusion of the ceremony, which was followed by a 21 gun salute by artillery guns. His horse, which had been very calm throughout the service, bolted at the first crack of the canon, and dashed through the the line of dignitaries, and across the cemetery with Foy clinging to the neck of the horse for dear life. It was, he said, his only close brush with death during the entire war.

After the war, with some of his army buddies, Foy succumbed to the allure of free land for veterans, took advantage of the Homestead Act, and staked a claim on land in Wyoming. This claim turned out to be in the midst of Wyoming's Oil Strike, but years after it had left his hands. The farmer's life was not to his liking, however, and after a year he accepted an offer to become a member of the band in a traveling circus. Soon he was a featured performer in the group, which toured throughout the midwest.

When the circus played in Plainview, sometime in 1922, a group of men from the Eden Valley community, northeast of Plainview, came to see the show. They were greatly impressed with ability of the young cornet player, and after the performance, approached him about coming to Eden Valley and helping them form a band. When the circus season was over Foy George did return and assembled a band from among the farmers in the Eden Valley area. This group proved to be hugely popular, and their success prompted some of the local business men to propose that George should organize a similar band in Plainview.

The new band was immediately appreciated, and Foy agreed to stay on in Plainview to become the permanent director of the Eden Valley and Plainview bands. His salary was to be paid by contributions from the business men and farmers of both communities. Amazingly, this arrangement worked out for almost two years, and the bands, made up entirely of men, young and old, prospered, and gained considerable respect in music circles throughout the area.

When George announced to the bands that he was to be married in 1924, a more dependable method of pay was needed, so a mill levy was passed. The taxpayers would pay his salary. This mill levy method of payment stayed in effect until Mr. George retired in 1964.

Soon the Eden Valley and the Plainview bands combined. But still the band was strictly a town band, with no connection to the school. An organized band of this type was something of a novelty and was in great demand for local events and celebrations throughout the area. Dr. Melerian, a local physician, organized a drive for uniforms and the members were quite dashing in blue and grey wool jackets with gold braid.

In 1924, Foy organized the band in the Plainview schools, which was reported to be one of the first such bands in the state. Both boys and girls constituted membership in the school band. Practices were held in the band room, in the basement of the old grade school building, across from B.E. Trump's Manual Training Room. Sometimes it was difficult to tell from which of these rooms those odd sounds were coming, whether it was a screeching clarinet or a whining buzz saw.

Also in 1924, Foy George was married to his high school sweetheart, Edna. She, like Foy, was a gifted musician. Her forte was vocal music. She had studied voice in Chicago and had sung solos, and with various groups in numerous concerts and radio programs in the Windy City. She was a beautiful young woman, with a promising career ahead of her, which she willingly gave up for marriage to the young band director. Their wedding pictures show a handsome young couple, eager to share their talents with the people of Plainview.

Soon after the Georges' marriage, and their settling in Plainview, Edna took sick with a debilitating disease and from that time until her death in 1964, she was confined to a wheel chair, with little or no control over her voice or limbs. Mr. George's sister-in-in-law and her daughter, Peggy, came to make their home with the Georges' and helped with Mrs. George during the 30's. The family was very self sufficient, and rarely required further help.

The band gained considerable local fame in the early years and entertained at various celebrations throughout the area. Probably the highlight of the early years was an hour's concert that the band was invited to present over Radio Station WOW in Omaha in 1925. The local group was reinforced with a number of good musicians from the surrounding towns for the occasion, and Foy performed as the featured soloist. When he told of the event years later, he laughed as he recalled that a delegation from Plainview had presented him with a brand new trumpet, in appreciation of his efforts with the band, and the Omaha concert was to be his first public appearance with the new horn. Everything went fine until half way through his first solo, when one valve started to stick, which caused him no end of grief, and resulted in a less than polished performance on his part. This may have had a lasting bearing on his solo work, because during the years I was in the band I never saw him perform alone.

The school band practiced before school on Monday, Wednesday, and Friday mornings and held regular concerts during the school year. They also played at the basketball and football games. Meanwhile, the Plainview Town band continued to perform as well. Practices for the Town Band were held on Monday nights throughout the year and the Town Band had regular concerts during the summer months on Friday nights. In the early years, at least, it was quite a prestigious thing for a school boy or girl to be asked to be in the Town Band and membership in that oranization was taken seriously, even though it involved extra practice to keep up with the "big guys".

Mr. George was a very patient man, with a well developed sense of humor. These attributes enabled him to cope with the antics of fledgling musicians for over 40 years. One time at a concert, Mr. George kept looking at two of the girls playing 2nd clarinet, with a frown on his face. At the end of the number he walked over and there was a brief, whispered conversation. It turned out that the two girls had turned two pages instead of one and had played the whole half of the number from music on the wrong page.

Another time Gordon Jewell, who was a cut up, but also a good trombone player, decided that he would insert a little excitement into a rehearsal. When Mr. George had to step out of the room for a few minutes Gordon lit up a cigarette and puffed up a storm. When Mr. George came back into the room he could smell the smoke, and called for the culprit to come forth and confess his crime. Of course no one moved. Mr. George sat down and announced that he would stay as long as it took. When the squirming got almost unbearable, Gordon finally came forward so that the rest of the group could go home. Though there was really no punishment, Mr. George and Gordon did have a little talk.

As the years went on, Mr. George began to use his own horn to play along with one or another section of the band that was having difficulty with a particular passage of music. To do this he played his trumpet out of the side of his mouth, fingering his instrument with his left hand, while he directed with his right. He got so that this was almost second nature to him and he could finger as well with his left hand as with his right. Curt Weatherhogg, a trumpet player in the band, got bored with the endless repetitions in learning a number. He decided that he could also learn to finger his trumpet with his left hand, and practiced at home until he managed quite well. Finally, he decided to demonstrate his skill at a rehearsal. Mr. George noticed Curt's left handed fingering and immediately stopped the band. He complimented Curt on his ingenuity, but told him how fingering with the left hand would cause the valves to seat themselves that way and would stick if you ever decided to go back to playing right handed. He added that Curt would do better to practice the music assigned in the prescribed manner.

Mr. George was extremely loyal, loyal to his family, and loyal to the people of Plainview. His thought was that the band belonged to the people, and ought to be available when the people requested the band's presence. In line with this philosophy, the band played for the opening of the Country Club each year, for the Community Free Day celebration, the Creamery Annual Meeting, and any other occasion that the city fathers felt called for band entertainment. On Memorial Day we played for the services at the cemetery, north of town. When I was first in the band we marched the one mile out and back, which prompted much grumbling, but later the lumber yards provided a couple of large flat bottomed trucks for our transportation--a great improvement.

In the summer the band played regular concerts on Friday nights. At first these concerts were in the large round bandstand in Chilvers Park, along Highway 20. This structure was originally built by the Home Guard. People would sit in their cars or on blankets on the ground to listen to the concerts. To get to the upper level we had to scale a narrow stairway, through a trap door in the floor. This was decidedly awkward for the tuba players and the bass drum. Once in place there was barely enough room for all the band.

One time Curt Weatherhogg and I had been caddying for a Ladies' Golf Tournament at the Country Club. The tournament was tied at the end of the day and our ladies had to play a couple of extra holes to determine a winner. That made us a little late getting back to town, and by the time we got to the park the band had already started to play. All we could do was wait until they finished the first number, then knock on the trap door for admittance. Mr. George didn't say a word as he lifted the door, but the look on his face was strong encouragement for us to be on time in the future.

One of my earliest recollections of the band at this old band stand was the playing of Sousa's Stars and Stripes Forever. I'm sure that the band played the number very well, but the reason that it stood out in my mind was because of the solo parts that were played by Joe Ruzicka, and Mr. Hughes. Joe probably weighed no more than 120 pounds, and played the big bass tuba. Mr. Hughes must have weighed nearly 300 pounds and played the piccolo. Standing side by side, playing their respective solos, they invariably brought down the house.

One summer "The Beer Barrell Polka" was the big rage. Friday after Friday we had that number on the program, till Mr. George announced that we were putting that selection away because he would go crazy if we played it one more time. We got through the Friday night program, were putting our instruments away, and had not played "Beer Barrell". But people did not leave. They honked and honked their horns, and the shouts of "Beer Barrell Polka" were insistent. Finally, Mr. George shook his head, and told us to get our horns back out of the cases and we played "Beer Barrell " not once but twice, and played it at every concert the rest of the season.

Because of Mrs. George's illness, Mr. George discouraged out of town trips. There were exceptions however. When the last segment was in place that resulted in linking Boston and Portland, making US Highway #20 a coast to coast "Super Highway", the

Plainview band took part in a huge parade and celebration in Sioux City.

Every year one day was designated as Plainview Day at the Pierce County Fair. The band always participated at the fair on this day. We played a concert in the grand stand, and then played for the acts on the stage. This was a bit of "old times" for Mr. George, and he brought out some of the music that he had used in his days with the circus. It was fun for us, but he did get a little exasperated because we were always getting interested in the acts and forgetting to play our horns. This was also the one time we got paid for playing. After we finished at the grandstand he would pass out $1 to each member which we could spend on the midway.

In addition to the band appearances, Mr George always had a small group, or music contest soloists who were available to provide a little entertainment. Good experience before the public, he called it. The ladies at the Women's Club and the WCTU must have been able to mark our progress as we made our annual appearance before their group.

I started in the band when I was in the 4th grade. At that time my folks bought a baritone from Jack Pubanz, for $25. It was a very heavy silver horn and was hard to blow. I did learn my notes on it and proved to my folks that I was serious about the band. Then we sold the horn back to Mr. Pubanz and arranged to buy a new baritone through Mr. George. This horn was a brass horn, much lighter and easier to blow. The total cost was $125. Soon after, one evening, about closing time, Mr. George came into the bakery for his usual loaf of bread and bag of cookies. Much to the shock of my dad, Mr. George gave him a check for $25, his commission for

97

selling us the horn. He said that he just appreciated having another horn in the band.

Mr. and Mrs. George were a familiar sight in Plainview. She still enjoyed music, and when the weather was good she would accompany him to the Monday night rehearsals. She sat in the car, outside an open window, and listened. Sometimes she would need some assistance. At these times she would manage to honk the horn, and Mr. George would go outside to tend to her needs. If he ever said one word of complaint or annoyance, I never heard it.

The Georges' liked the movies. I'm sure that they attended almost every change of picture, which in those days ran Sunday-Monday-Tuesday, changed Wednesday-Thursday, and again Friday-Saturday. They always sat in the same place, on the right hand side, a little more than half way to the front, beside the emergency exit. Mr. George would bring Mrs. George through this door 15 minutes or so before the picture started, then park his car in the alley. After the picture they would slip out this same exit, and avoid the crowd.

For a few years in the 30's Mr. George had a small camping trailer which he deemed suitable for their vacation travel. Driving in the car was one thing that Mrs. George could do and liked to do. He had wanted to visit Buffalo, Wyoming, and the site of his land claim, and also Yellowstone Park. Having no experience pulling a trailer, he embarked on self taught course. He spent several days at the football field, practicing backing his trailer through the goal posts, around pylons, and hooking up and unhooking the rig from his car.

Mr. George was a very modest man, and there was some criticism directed toward him for not being very flashy with the band. Yet, this was the man that started the marching band at football games, and worked out the maneuvers on graph paper before teaching them to the band on the football field. Later he added the majorettes. To teach the majorettes to twirl the baton, he first had to learn to twirl the baton himself. There were plenty of eager young majorette hopefuls who soon surpassed him in twirling skills, and they were able to convince the mothers to sew the first majorette costumes.

The first school uniforms were purchased sometime in the early 30's. They consisted of red gabardine jackets, with a minimum of white trim, and brass buttons, white trousers and red overseas caps. By the time I joined the band in the mid 30's the jackets had been washed so often that they were decidedly limp, and they didn't always fit very well. Mr. George was definitely the sharpest member of the band in his all white woolen director's suit with gold braid, brass buttons and matching garrison cap.

Mr. George was a marvelous story teller, and especially enjoyed telling stories where he was the butt of the joke. He told of his trip to Wyoming with the trailer. He especially wanted to see the site of his old claim, which was right in the midst of the great Wyoming oil fields, though of course it had been out of his hands for years. "Selling the land too soon was just one of his many mistakes", he said. In one of the small towns they had a bit of car trouble. While the car was being fixed the garage owner invited Foy over to the tavern for a little afternoon refreshment. They joined a group at one of the tables, and the waitress said that she would bring them their regular order. Foy, who regularly partook of one of the Hill brothers' great malted milks and drank liquor never, this time thought that to be one of the boys he should order a beer in this bar. When the order came, Foy got his beer and each of the others got a chocolate malted milk.

In the late 30's, as a WPA project, the new band shell was constructed in what was called the Athletic Park. This was a great facility, and the accoustics were much improved over the old round band stand. The Band Shell is now listed in the Registry of Historic Buildings. From that time on this was the home of the Friday night concerts. For some reason, Mr. George never cared to announce the numbers from the stage. This task fell to Joe Ruzicka, who enjoyed the duty immensley. At first he used a megaphone which he would direct in each direction. Later, with the addition of the sound system he could make his announcements from his position in the back row of the band.

In 1961, to commemorate the 75th anniversary of the incorporation of Plainview, Plainview grad, Bob (Roberts) Warren, of the TV show "This Is Your Life" returned home to honor three of Plainview's favorite people. Mr. George was one of the honorees chosen to be the subject of a "This Is Your Life" show. It was fitting that the show took place on the stage of Mr. George's band stand in the park.

In 1964, the same year that Mrs. George passed away, Mr. George retired from teaching and directing the school band and the Town band, after some 42 years in Plainview. To mark this occasion a committee was formed which raised the funds to present Mr. George with a new car, one more gesture of thanks for a job well done.

Though there were numerous times that the band caused Mr. George a considerable degree of exasperation, I only saw him really mad just once. It was a beautiful day in early spring and at noon everyone was rushing to go home for lunch. A couple of upperclass boys from the country (the country boys and girls were the only ones who drove to school) had taken their brown bag lunches and jumped into their car and roared away from the curb. By the time they got to the end of the block they were going quite fast. At that moment a little girl from the grade school was crossing the street. The girl had a crippled leg and got around, slowly, with the aid of crutches. Instead of slowing, the driver bore down on her, swerving at the last moment, while the girl fell to the ground, in her haste to get back onto the curb. Both boys in the car were laughing at her misfortune as they sped away--- just as Mr. George was coming out of the grade school building.

Fortunately, the little girl was unhurt, and there were other students, as well as Mr. George, to help her to her feet. When the boys came back after noon, Mr. George was waiting for them outside their home room. He backed them against the wall and proceeded to give the bullies a blistering lecture they would never forget, to the point that one of the boys was reduced to tears. That still did not end the incident. At the next band practice, Mr. George stopped the rehearsal and told us of the incident. He didn't use the boys' or the girl's names, but in a small school it wasn't necessary. Everyone already knew. He told us how we must be constantly grateful of our own normal bodies. Then he told how it was to be handicapped, to be dependent upon someone else for everything that had to be done. And just because

101

someone was handicapped, physically, it didn't mean that he didn't understand, that he could not think. Manytimes the handicapped liked the same things we did, but had to do things, enjoy things, in a little bit different way. As members of the same Human Race, it was our duty to help those with handicaps, not to put further obstacles in their way. It was a stirring speech, delivered from the heart. I doubt if anyone who was at band practice that day has forgotten it.

Foy George 1896-1968

WALTER'S CANARY CAGES

My Dad, Walter, is what you would call a fiscal conservative, and "close with the buck". At 92, I guess he's never going to change that handle. But I think he comes by this trait naturally. He was the youngest of eight children of German immigrants who settled in the arid west river country in South Dakota in the late 1890's. The family attempted to wrest a living from a land claim near Oacoma, S.D., and for several years fought the battle of drought and grasshoppers to a near draw. But after a few townspeople heard that his father, Richard, had baking experience back in Germany, they persuaded him to start a bakery in Oacoma. (soon after he moved the bakery to Presho.)

In the early days of the century a large family was a definite asset in the operation of a business. This was especially true of the bakery business. In the bakery there is always a need for another pair of hands, even young hands, and all of the Sehnert children assisted in various ways in the work of the family bakery. Walter learned the value of work, and the basics of the bakery trade at a very early age.

When World War I broke out Walter's older brothers left to join the army and eventually wound up fighting in France. The younger boys, Walter and Rudy, were too young for the army and with the three sisters they assisted their parents in family business, which by this time included a restaurant and small hotel.

After the war, when the family again established contact with relatives in Germany they learned what can happen to "money" when inflation goes rampant, as happened in post-war Germany during the 1920's. A relative in Germany wrote that the German mark lost value so fast that it literally was not worth as much as the paper on which it was printed. Since most of the uncles still in Germany were in the bakery business they were relatively unhurt by the inflationary pressures that the country was facing. The value of their bread inflated along with other commodities and they were able to remain afloat, though of course times were very hard. They told of one friend, a farmer, who owed money on his land. One day he brought a basket of eggs to the bank. He and the banker agreed that each egg had reached the value of several thousands of marks. So after considerable haggling, the farmer gave the banker the basket of eggs, which represented real value, and the banker gave him back the mortgage on his farm--debt paid in full.

My folks, Walter and Lenita, bought the bakery in Plainview in 1930. Times were hard in the 30's and banks were beginning to fail across the country. Plainview was not spared this catastrophe. At one time there had been a bank on each corner of the main intersection. By 1933 there was but one, in the location where the bank, now the Plainview National Bank, presently stands. There was even a "run" on that bank, but its reserves were such that it was able to remain open. Ben Saunders, the president of the bank at that time, later came to Walter and thanked him his vote of confidence in not asking to take his money out of the bank during the crisis. Walter said later that he had so little money in the bank that it really made very little difference if he took it out or not. He wasn't sure how he would have reacted had his account been sizeable.

Then there was one more incident that had a big impact on Walter's thoughts on the accumulation of money. On a trip to South Dakota, a brother-in-law talked him into investing in a gold mine in the area of the Black Hills. Now everyone knows that there is indeed gold in "them thar hills", but somehow the contact of the brother-in-law's was shifty in setting up the deal, and that paper, the "gold mine shares" turned out to be worthless. Fortunately they did not represent any great deal of money, but the experience, nevertheless, was painful and memorable.

The lesson that Walter learned from all this: Wealth is only represented by something that you can see and touch, or walk on. He has, of course, come to trust banks to a certain extent, though I'm sure he would prefer to carry his money in his billfold. But he really feels that true wealth is land, with its buildings, crops, and livestock. Everything else is an illusion that might be gone tomorrow.

Young men are indeed fortunate if they can have a mentor to whom they can turn for advice, and Walter, in the 30's, had a good one. Frank Holbert had been the president of one Plainview banks, which failed with the stock market crash of 1929. When Walter and Lenita came to Plainview, he was in the insurance/real estate business . He liked the young couple and frequently talked to them about their goals and what they should be working toward. As soon as they could scrape together a down payment he helped them to buy a farm south of Plainview. This was truly the start of the grand experience of Walter's life, the owning of land, stocking it with livestock, rubbing elbows with farmers, and solving the problems of agriculture over innumerable cups of coffee at Mary's Cafe.

When Walter became a landowner he started going to farm sales, where he began to buy the animals and equipment needed for a successful farm operation. In those days Dean Mosher was a leading local auctioneer and called many of the farm sales. He and Walter were friends and he frequently made Walter the butt of the jokes he used to liven up a sale. One time there were three bird cages on a sale that Dean tried and tried to sell, but failed to get a single bid. Finally, in desperation, he said "Sold to Walt Sehnert for 25 cents!" though Walter had not opened his mouth. Everyone had a good laugh and Walter took the bird cages to the farm and stored them in the barn. After that, at every sale where there was a bird cage, Dean would only make the flimsiest try for a sale, then conclude "Sold to Walt Sehnert for 25 cents".

The procedure got to be a running gag, and even when Walter was not at a sale Dean would buy the bird cage himself so that he could pass it off on Walter at his next sale. The gag climaxed at a sale where there were a half dozen bird cages, no buyers, and Dean was able to unload the whole bunch for the usual 25 cents.

Then in 1944, Walter had a farm sale of his own, where he sold livestock, machinery and items he had picked up at numerous farm sales. It was a cold day in February, and Dean was hurrying the sale along as best he could. When he was almost finished with the small items Walter had the men bring out a wagon completely loaded with bird cages, 22 in number. (I know because it had been my job to assemble them and clean them up for the sale.) When Dean Mosher saw all of those bird cages he burst out laughing as did the rest of the regular sale goers who had followed the gag over the years. His comment was "Now how in hell am I going to sell these bird cages when I don't have Walt Sehnert to unload on?" But he manfully made the attempt, and started the bidding at, what else, 25 cents.

Sometimes providence smiles, even on a cold day in February. On that particular day it so happened that a lady from the Creighton area had decided to go into the business of raising canaries for sale to pet shops. Her business had grown to the extent that she had run out of bird cages and had heard that there might be some available at this sale. Now this would have been wonderful, to be able to finally get rid of the bird cages at all, but wonder of wonders, that day there was also a lady from around Norfolk who had recently gotten into the business of raising parakeets, and she too had need for more bird cages. So these two ladies began bidding against one another. The bidding was spirited, and eventually the bid got to over $5.00 per cage. At that point Dean thought that he had gotten enough. He stopped the sale and worked out a compromise, whereby the ladies each took half the cages and the sale moved on to other items.

A few days after the sale Dean Mosher came up to Walter in the coffee shop and said, "You have got to be the luckiest so and so in this county. I'm not going to let you get a monopoly on anything again. If you start collecting harness sets I'll believe that the horse and buggy is coming back into style. You buy the coffee for the house today!"

THE ENTREPRENEUR

It was in Mabel Trump's high school English class. The word "entrepreneur" came up and Mickie White wanted to know what the word meant. Mabel explained that an entrepreneur was someone who recognized a business opportunity, seized the opportunity, then worked to make the business a success. Mabel added that a true entrepreneur tended move from one opportunity to another, and added that he should by all means have an understanding wife. From the back of the room, "Gee, that sounds like your Dad, Mickie!"

Certainly, Plainview has had its share of entrepreneurs. Plainview's first settlers were entrepreneurs of the first order. There were men who came to Plainview and probably amassed larger fortunes. And we had men from Plainview who left town and became wildly successful in various entrepreneurial pursuits. These men generally stuck with their main endeavor and added other ventures. But for my period, of the 30's and 40's, Maurice White does indeed fit the definition of an entrepreneur; one who saw opportunities, changed directions, took chances, and succceeded, all in Plainview. (And had an understanding wife)

Maurice White was a little man, shorter than his wife, but a man of great energy. He had come to Plainview in the early 30's, from Foster, where he had been a barber. He arrived with a wife, Leila, three kids, and little more than his sisscors and comb. He barbered for a time in Plainview, in Harley Hawk's Barber Shop, but it couldn't have been very long, because by the time I was five or six, I remember him as the owner of the

Corner Cafe, across from Steinkraus Oil and a few doors west of our apartment, above the bakery, on Locust Street. The cafe was tiny, but the whole family worked to make it a success. They served good food and were very busy. Mrs. White was relieved that Maurice had gotten into something that provided the family a living.

The three White children were among my first friends. All of them had inherited their dimunutive statures from their father. Verona, five years older than I, was already helping her folks in the cafe. At that time I considered her "big sister bossy" and I'm sure she considered us pests. We teased her about her boyfriends.

Bob was three years older, and though I might have chosen to spend more of my time with him, he was busy with older friends and generally was successful in evading my attempts to be his "buddy".

Mickie, born Myrtle Ellen, and I were the same age. Since we both spent so much time downtown we became, with Betty Cox, whose mother cooked for the Whites, best pals. We started school in the same class when the that time came. This was, of course, in those early childhood years, before the ages of 7-13, at which time boys are compelled to only associate with boys.

When I was in the 2nd grade our family moved out of the bakery apartment and into a house across from the bandshell park on North Main Street. The Whites took our place in the apartment above the bakery. In the process of moving Mrs. White congratulated my mother on our new house, and expressed that her dream was that they, too, would have a house of their own someday. My mother assured her that such would certainly happen, and Mrs. White was always pleased that some years later, when they built their house at the west end of Locust Street, my mother was the first visitor to her new home.

When we were in Jr. High School, and things were going well at the Corner Cafe, Maurice suprised everyone by selling the cafe. He had spotted an opportunity, and soon announced that he was putting in a tavern in the building next to Ebinger Hardware. The place was known as "The Pine Room", and featured walls faced with highly polished knotty pine wallboard. This place immediately became a popular "Watering Hole" in Plainview.

At that age, I did not have much contact with the Pine Room, except for one short period of time when Maurice installed two Duck Pin alleys in the basement of the tavern. Duck Pins was very much like regular bowling, except that there were only nine pins to be knocked down and the ball one used was much smaller than a regular bowling ball. It was a fun game, but the location was wrong. The basement quarters were cramped, and the ventilation was non-existant. In those heavy smoking days the air quickly became so polluted that it was difficult to see the pins at the other end of the alley. The project was soon abandoned, which pleased Mickie as her Saturday shift regularly made her late in joining the gang at Baber's Cafe for Cokes and dancing.

These were good years for the the Whites, and it was during this time that they were able to build their new home. At last Mrs. White could relax, thinking that finally their course on the road to success was set. It must have been a bit of a shock when Maurice announced, in 1944, that he had sold the Pine Room.

Maurice, anticipating a great demand for automobiles once the war ended, announced that he had acquired a

Chrysler Agency, and was erecting a modern garage and salesroom on the lots south of their home on Locust St.

At that time there was a government imposed ceiling on what a dealer could charge for a new car, though the demand for any new or good used car was huge. The common practice of the day was for a dealer to sell a car for the ceiling price, but accept a little "sweetener under the table".

Maurice announced that as soon as the new cars were released, we would be able to buy Plymouths and Chryslers from him, at list price. After four long years without new cars, this was exciting news indeed.

When the war ended there was a long list of people who had signed up for a the first new car from the new Chrysler Agency. It must have been with mixed feelings that Maurice turned over the keys for a beautiful new blue Chrysler to Earhardt Hemmingsen, only to see Earhardt drive the car across the street and sell it to someone else for a handsome profit. Earhardt said later that he could surely afford to drive his old car a little longer for that kind of money.

Maurice worked hard to learn the automobile business in a short time. The Chrysler Agency was certainly sussessful, and life for Mrs. White was a bit more leisurely, but later, when he had the chance, he closed out the Chrysler Agency and bought out Saathoff's Chevrolet Agency and moved it into his building at the end of Locust Street, no doubt feeling in his entrepreurial heart that the GM product line offered the better opportunity and better reward.

My only real contact with Maurice White, the auto dealer, didn't come until I was at the University of Nebraska. I had been working summers and had saved about $600, and thought that I needed a car. It just happened that Maurice had what I considered the perfect car, a little white 1940 expanded Chevy coupe. The problem was that he was asking $900.

We talked at length about the car, and he agreed to alter the transmission to update it, but I could not get him to come down on the price. Some of my friends assured me that I only needed to be firm and he would at least split the difference.

Finally, as I turned to leave the showroom for the last time, sure enough, Maurice called me back. I was elated. "To get this deal moving", he said, "I'm willing come down on the price. I'll knock $25 off the price of that car. What do you say?"

My jaw must have dropped a foot. I was arguing for a reduction of hundreds and he was offering me $25.

I fear that I left the garage that day in a considerable huff. I did what I always did in a crisis. I went to the bakery to talk to my Dad. When he heard the story he started to laugh. "That sounds just like Maurice", he said. "I've been doing business, back and forth, with him since we came to town, and I can tell you that you are not going beat him in a deal. And he's not going to give you any favors. But I also know that if he is asking you $900 for that car he is pretty sure that he's going to be able to get $900 for that car, and if you want it you'd better take it now and be happy for the $25 discount. You can also be sure that if it doesn't perform as he says, he'll make it right."

So, with Dad's help I bought the car. It turned out to be a great car, and I was never sorry about our deal. Sometimes entrepreneurs really are OK.

Lunch with the Governor

I was reminded of an amusing incident the other day while having lunch with the Governor.... There, that ought to take care of at least a year of name dropping. The truth is, I'm not a big buddy of the Nebraska's Governor Nelson, nor am I somebody that he calls upon to help him make momentous decisions of state. He is from McCook, and he had his first job, as a 16 year old, at our bakery. We have remained friends over the years and we, at the bakery, have been privileged to help him remember his mother on many occasions with decorated cakes and other goodies. He also chose to kick off his campaign for Governor at our bakery. This time I was in attendance at a luncheon at the Governor's Mansion as a stand-in for my son who had won the luncheon at a fund raiser for the Heart Association.

The Governor's mother happened to be visiting from McCook and joined us for lunch. She recalled incidents, which I remembered well, such as Benny's first day at the bakery. He was surprised when we assured him that he might eat all of the donuts he desired as they came, still hot, from the glazer. She remembered that he took full advantage of the situation and O.D'd (over do-nutted) that first morning, and never abused the privilege again. She also remembered how the kids at school had teased him about being Mr. Donut, a reference to the smell of donuts that permeated his clothing and clung to him as he passed from class to class during the morning.

At the McCook bakery, in years past, we had a shift where school boys would arrive at 4:30 in the morning. They would assist the bakers on the bench, fry the donuts, deliver baked goods to the restaurants, and assist in some cleanup of the bakery until they left for school. In Plainview the shift was a little different, but in each case the boys had to work quickly and well at a responsible position during the time they were on the job. They were an important part of our crew, and we would not have been able to keep the bakery going without them. Over the years I suppose that we had hundreds of these young men on the payroll, and I know that many times we were instrumental in the purchase of their first car (along with the oppressive insurance costs to which young men are subjected). On the way home from the Governor's Mansion that day I began to think about these young fellows.

Governor Ben told us about being invited to participate in the "High speed Automobile Chase Course" that the Nebraska State Patrol uses in their training program. He remarked that he had gone through that course at high speed, knocking down only one pylon, a feat that was considered very good. Immediately I began to wonder if part of that skill had not been learned by striving to complete his restaurant deliveries in our bakery truck and still get to school on time. As far as I ever knew, Ben did not abuse his driving privileges while he worked at the bakery.

That is not to say that all of the boys were always as careful. We had our share of accidents, fortunately none too serious, over the years. Once Johnny Logan lost control of the bakery truck near Brunswick, and rolled the vehicle as he attempted to to protect himself from a bumble bee. Another time Leo Steinkraus, certainly no teenager, sideswiped a train coming back from Wausa, and miraculously walked away from that mishap with only a scraped fender and damaged pride.

On one occasion, in McCook, a young man was making deliveries with our family car, as the bakery truck was temporarily out of commission. He had made a delivery to the sale barn and decided to make a little detour on a back road, to see what the boss's old jalopy could do. He never did say how fast he was going, but when he hit a bit of loose gravel the car spun out of control and he landed in the ditch, unhurt, but shaken. When I arrived at the scene of the accident, the city policeman was already there. He had our delivery boy with his hands on the car and he was on the radio. He was telling the dispatcher that he needed help, as he suspected alcohol and drugs. He was new in McCook, and was not aware of the bakery's system, in which we picked up beer and soft drink flats (the shallow cardboard container that holds 4 six packs of beer or pop) from the cafes and bars, then recycled them with wax paper and plastic overwraps into containers for sweet rolls for our deliveries to the restaurants. He mistook all of those beer flats as signs of a huge beer party, and suspected that alcohol was responsible for the accident (at 7:30 a.m.). That was one time that I really got mad, not at the delivery boy (that came later), but at that policeman. I fear that I gave him a piece of my mind for being so dense that he could not see what was perfectly obvious. This young man had merely decide to take a little joy ride, and had gone too fast. While he was dumb for doing this it did not mean that he was drunk or on drugs. And furthermore, I thought that the law ought to give credit to a young man who had enough ambition to get up early to go a responsible job before school, and they should not immediately suspect him of that sort of spurious behavior. In the end, after talking with his superiors, the officer did apologize for jumping to conclusions and we eventually became quite good friends.

I really did respect these young men for their drive and work ethic. Getting up alone while the world sleeps is not easy, and night work is much more difficult than working days. In Plainview, Lloyd Carstens was introduced to bakery work under the most difficult circumstance possible. At 9 or 10 o'clock in the evening preceding one of Plainview's Free Days (one of the busiest days of the year for the bakery) my Dad offered Lloyd a job, to fill in for one of the bakers who did not show up for work. Lloyd accepted and worked from that hour until the middle of the next afternoon. Not being used to the work, and after no rest from the day before, he must have been dead on his feet. It is a small miracle that he ever came back to the bakery again. But come back he did, and remained for almost 40 years, until my Dad sold out the Plainview bakery, becoming, over the years, a fine baker, a loyal employee, and a good friend.

Of course, not all of the young men who came to work were good workers, and not all of the good workers stayed. One poor fellow never could get used to the night hours. He was regularly late for work, and one time that he had left home on time, we found him parked outside the bakery, fast asleep, still sitting up, behind the wheel of his car. He could sleep standing up. This was not so bad when he was working at the bench, as the bakers would help him wake up by dropping a large baking sheet on the floor, or hit the bench sharply with a rolling pin, both sounds resounding like a gunshot, but one time he fell asleep while he was frying donuts and allowed his

116

hand to drop into the hot grease. That was the last straw, and we mutually decided that he would be better off taking a day job.

Once a young man came to work for my Dad who had an attitude problem, coupled with a loose tongue. Whatever Dad told him to do he would argue and grumble under his breath when Dad turned his back. In those days my Dad had a rather short temper, and on a particular day when this fellow was glazing donuts he said something that Dad could not tolerate. Dad turned back to the fellow and grasped him by the shirt collar and the seat of his pants and proceeded to bodily throw him out the door. Certainly, the fellow was promptly and properly fired, but since he had his hands in the liquid donut glaze there was a path of sugary syrup on the machinery, the walls and even the ceiling, all the way to the front door. For the rest of the morning there was silence in the bakery. No one wanted to cross my Dad, and everyone strove to clean walls and machinery in between their other tasks. Only as people were getting ready to leave for the day was there any expression of mirth as people began to describe just how the scene unfolded, and told of their amazement that my Dad, just a little fellow, could perform such a feat.

Governor Nelson is a fine example of the "good guys" we've had at the bakery. He's the only one of our "boys" who has become Governor, though I'm sure that if some others had decided on a political career they might have made it. Several of the fellows have become lawyers, and one is now a judge. One of the surprises is the young man who became an FBI agent. One is a executive for a large company which does business internationally. Another is the president of a college.

Only one fellow, to my knowledge, besides my son, has his own bakery. I'm not really sure why this is. I fear that it has something to do with my deficiencies as a teacher and motivator. One fellow became my son-in-law, and I consider his training at the bakery to be an important part of his maturation. Several of the fellows have their own small businesses, and have sympathized, in later years, with me over our mutual help problems, and they have regretted the "hard time" they gave me while they were on the bakery payroll. In McCook, a railroad town, many of the boys have gone on to become railroaders and others work in various jobs around town. Frequently they thank me for the experience of working at the bakery, and my introducing them to those "wee hours" of the morning, which they say helps them to overcome the tedium of their present job. They know that something could be worse.

In describing this bit of the past I am struck by the realization that all of these young people I've mentioned are young men. In those days now past there were no young women working those early hours. But alas, those days are over. We have not had young men working that early, donut frying shift for a number of years. We had increasing trouble finding young men to fill that position and for the last years have been hiring their mothers, and older sisters. The turnover in personnel has decreased to almost nil, and in truth we have experienced far less troubles. But I still think about that legion of young men who passed through the bakery. They brought a certain excitement with them, a refreshing zest for life, an uncertainty of what the day would bring. I learned a lot from them. I thank them all. I wish them well. I wouldn't have missed it for the world.

MABEL AND B.E.

Note: The lives of Mabel and B.E. Trump in Plainview are divided into two parts, namely their early careers as teachers, and their later careers as successful operators of the greehouse business in Plainview. The following account covers only their teaching years. W.S.

Mabel and B.E. and the Plainview School System. For those of us who went to school in Plainview during the 20's, 30's, and 40's, these two institutions were synonymous. Mabel and B.E. Trump came to Plainview in the early 20's, and served in various capacities in the Plainview High School and Junior High until they retired to open their greenhouse business in the early 50's.

Byron Estel Trump was born in Felicity, Ohio, in 1893, the son of a Methodist minister. Later, his father accepted a call to serve churches in Shoals and Randolph, Nebraska, and Estel, as the family referred to him, finished his education at Randolph High School and Wayne State Normal College. His first teaching assignment was at a high school in western Iowa. He was hired to teach math and science in the school, but the school also needed a basketball coach. Though Estel had not played basketball, he had read a book on the subject. This was recommendation enough for him to get the job. He must have done a credible coaching job, as one of his teams went all the way to the Iowa High School State Basketball finals.

When World War I began, B.E., as he was now known, entered the US Army, and served in France. He saw considerable action during the war, and during one raid he was caught in a poison gas attack, which injured his lungs and led to a medical discharge. Though he

119

recovered sufficiently to resume his teaching careeer, he never did entirely regain his full health, and suffered chronic lung ailments for the rest of his life.

After leaving the army he came back to Nebraska and taught school in some of the small schools around Wayne, NE for a few years, until he took a position as science teacher at Creighton, NE. At Creighton he was a popular teacher, and worked well with his students. Radio was just coming into popularity, and there were kits available for young people to assemble their own radio sets. B.E. got permission from the school authorities to help his students build their radios at school, but only after school hours. Things went along just fine until one of the school board members discovered that the students were also using school electricity to make their radios work, each using the equivalent of a 20 watt lightbulb. This was too much, and B.E.was told to stop his project. B.E. stopped, but at the same time tendered his resignation from the Creighton school and accepted a similar position in the Plainview Schools.

By this time Mabel Hansen, four years younger than B.E. had finished her college work at Wayne State Normal College and was teaching in a rural school near Wayne. By her own account, and substantiated by first hand accounts of fellow students and year book records, Mabel had an outstanding college career, both in the classroom and in extra curricular activities, especially speech and drama.

Her drama accomplishments were easy to believe, as she invariable made a dramatic entrance into every classroom or meeting she entered, and projected her words to a class as if she were delivering lines of a play to an audience. Over many years she produced, directed, and promoted countless stage plays in the community and the high school. These productions were popular, and the townspeople could look forward to an entertaining evening, attending one of her plays. Aspiring young actors, from the Junior and Senior classes, competed for roles in the plays with the same enthusiasm as did the athletes trying out for the basketball team. Along the way, the students did learn a bit of discipline, the fundamentals of putting on a play, and had a lot of fun in the process.

Mabel and B.E. had already planned to be married when B.E. took the Plainview assignment. This was in the early 20's. Soon after B.E. accepted his new position, Mabel traveled by train to Plainview to visit B.E. and look over the town. Years later she told of getting off the train in Plainview. "The wind was blowing hard, and there were no trees. The town looked so desolate I just broke down and bawled like a baby. I promised myself that I would stay one year, for B.E.'s sake, but after that I was getting back to civilization!" Instead, she stayed for the rest of her life.

Mabel was a rather tall, raw boned woman, with never changing auburn hair. B.E. was somewhat shorter, and completely bald. Mabel was always in a hurry, and walked into a room as if she were charging a fortress. B.E. sauntered. He never seemed to be in a hurry, and as a consequence, frequently walked a pace or two behind his wife. They lived in the block south of our house, when I knew them, one house north of the Ebinger home (now the Gene Steinkraus home) on Main Street. They had a small English bulldog which some neighborhood wags said resembled B.E., and which Mabel treated like

121

her child, talking to it in baby talk, picking it up and snuggling it with great affection. These same wags said that Mabel treated that little bulldog with a lot more affection and respect that she did B.E.

It is true that Mabel did criticize B.E. often times in public. She would make her demands, theatrically, and admonish him to wait on her more than some of us thought was necessary. But B.E. did not seem to notice that he was being put upon, and did her bidding with good grace, though silently, and at his own pace.

One time the two of them were taking several of us Boy Scouts to a camp near Fremont in the old Whippet(?) automobile. At the time, I'm sure that it was the largest car in town. It was not new, but it was quite grand, and very much suited Mabel's personality. The story was that she had won the car in a contest, selling subscriptions the the Norfolk Daily News, and since they were not financially able to afford another, newer car of that caliber, they continued to drive the old one.

On this trip Mabel had been nagging B.E. since we left Plainview, over some rather trivial matter, the nature of which I've forgotten. The matter would appear to be settled, only to be reopened after a few miles. B.E. was driving and would grunt, or shrug, or mumble at her diatribe, but never did cross her. Still she kept bringing her grievance up. Finally B.E. could take it no longer. He turned to her, raised his voice ever so slightly, and said, "Mom, shut up!", and turned back to his driving. Mabel stopped in mid-sentence, as if she had been struck. She looked at him for a long moment, then started to cry. "Why, Daddy, you don't need to yell at me. I don't think you love me any more." The argument was settled.

Both B.E. and Mabel were active in civic affairs and were officers in the Eastern Star lodge, as well as many other organizations in the community. One of her positions, which she held for many years, was that of leader of the Girl Scouts, and very often she took her girls on a summer campout at Yellowbanks, a popular camping site at the time, near Norfolk. She took it upon herself to teach the girls not only the skills of camp and crafts, but also the social graces and good grammar (always grammar) that she felt would be useful to young ladies during their lifetimes.

B.E. also led the Boy Scout Troop #162 during the time I was in the organization. This was during the period of time leading up to WWII, and in the early months of the war. During the war years the scout movement went downhill. B.E. became too busy with his school duties, other leaders were hard to find, and, with the world in turmoil, there just seemed to be things that were more important than scouting.

When B.E. had the troop we met in the band room of the old grade school building. It was a fine place to meet, and sometimes we would get out our intruments to play a little music. B.E.'s Manual Training Room was across the hall, and he would often take us over there to work on a scout project or just to teach us how to use one or another of the woodworking tools.

In the summer we would have small overnight campouts, where we worked on merit badge projects, scouting techniques, and always had a lot of fun. A favorite place for these campouts was in the Dufek Grove, north and west of town, on the way to the Country Club. Once we camped there on a Saturday night. Some of us were old enough that we missed the activities of a

Saturday night in town. After lights out we plotted to skip out for awhile, walk to town, play a little pool, and get back while B.E. slept in his tent. He would never know we had been gone.

We walked the three miles to town and played our pool at Homer's Poolhall, then talked my Dad into taking us back to the campsite. We had him drop us off a half mile away, and we slipped silently back into the camp, undetected. B.E. never did say anything about our being gone, but I was always sure that our guilty consciences were so glaring that he just must have known.

One of the last Boy Scout ceremonies that I remember B.E. presiding over, was a public convocation commemorating Boy Scout Week. We were in the high school gym and there were a lot of people in attendance (or so it seemed to me). We were taking in some new members. Each of us older scouts chose one of the Scout Laws, and we were to give that law from memory. Then we were to all give the Scout Oath in unison, as an example to the new members---an impressive climax to the ceremony.

All had gone well, and each of us had done quite a commendable job of reciting our Law from memory. Because he was the oldest of our group, Kenny Dickinson was given the honor of giving the last law, "A Scout is Trustworthy". He looked very fine, in his uniform, as he stepped forward to begin his little speech. And he began, "A Scout is Trusworthy, he always strives...". He began again, "A Scout is Trustworthy, he always strives..., he always strives to..., to..., to..., Oh hell, I can't remember!" And he turned and walked off the stage, and out of scouting. B.E., himself, gave up his post as Scoutmaster shortly after that.

124

Mabel considered herself a grammarian and a parliamentarian. She had no hesitation in correcting her students for using the wrong word, the wrong syntax, or a commonly used vulgar expression at any time, whether they were at the moment in her class or not. Even as adults her former students were not above reprimand. In her various organizations she was insistent that the meeting procede according to "Roberts Rules of Order", even though this often meant numerous interruptions for "Point of Order!" (and groans from the other members of the group).

Mabel could be quite stern with her students. She carried herself with an air of dignity and prided herself on the discipline she maintained in her class room. In reading passages of literature to her class she would regularly, without looking up from her text, single out a student for reprimand, and announce, "Peggy Holmes(frequently), stop that!", knowing full well that Peggy, if not actively engaged in mischief at the moment, soon would be.

But she liked to have a good time with her students as well. In one of her classes students were talking when they should have been listening. After warning them, once, she lowered the boom, and announced that the guilty people would have to stay after school and write "I will not talk in class" 500 times. When the punishment began, one student complained that writing that sentence 500 times would be a waste of time, and could he not write an essay of the equivalent number of words, on his autobiography. Mabel thought that this might be agreeable. Of course when the student got into the subject he got interested in the prose he was submitting, and wrote a paper, following the rules that had been taught in class. Mabel corrected the paper, offered encouragement, along with suggestions, and they laughed together over the incidents presented.

Mabel, the taskmaster, also had her "pets" in the class room. One of these "pets" was John Andresen, a fellow who was rather casual with all persons in authority. One time we were working on a play, or some other project, after school hours. Mabel had been expounding on some subject, and mentioned that she and B.E. had separate bedrooms. Later on, she was speaking about rearing children. She said she regretted that she and B.E. had never had any children of their own. John piped up, observing that they might have had children, had it not been for those separate bedrooms. Mabel answered him, in her most theatric manner, "That, sir, is certainly not the case. B.E. made that trip so often he wore a path in the carpet and we had to have it replaced!" End of discussion.

In Mabel, B.E. got a wife who liked nice things. She prided herself on the fine woolen suits she ordered from the Pendleton Mills in Oregon (and never seemed to go out of style), her fur coats, and the silver and china she used at her elaborate dinner parties. B.E., on the other hand was comfortable in more casual attire. At school, instead of a suit coat, he often wore a heavy red coat sweater from his Iowa coaching days. And at home he was most comfortable puttering in his shop or garden. In those lean days of the 30's they must have been on a very limited budget, but they managed well, and were considered among the elite of Plainview. They treasured their free time in the summers and for years they traveled to Colorado or Wyoming, to camp in the mountains. Their interests were many and varied and they

126

thoroughly enjoyed the life they had chosen for themselves.

The years of World War II had to a be most trying time for the Trumps. This was a time of sacrifice, and along with everyone else, they were asked to do more, and they did it. It was the patriotic thing to do. As teachers left the school system, either by way of the draft or natural attrition, replacements were not readily available. Former teachers were called out of retirement. Current teachers took on additional classes, often outside their chosen field. Mabel and B.E. certainly shouldered their share of the load. B.E. took over the high school principal's duties, assisted in the basketball coaching, and taught a full schedule of classes. In 1943 the Trumps were saddled with the entire administrative duties, when B.E. was named superintendent, and Mabel was named Principal of the high school, between the tenures of John Weaterhogg and A.G. Petersen.

Most of the former teachers who returned to the classroom did a fine job of keeping the system going, but it must be said that some were really not able to handle their assignment. We had a typing teacher, for instance, who tended to fall asleep at inopportune times. Once, during a one minute timed typing test, she dropped off, and slept until she was awakened by the bell, at the end of the class period. Needless to say, the typing rates for that particular test were spectacular, and helped our averages considerably. However, the next time we had our typing test, B.E. managed to be on hand to supervise our class and the test himself.

Both B.E. and Mabel managed to insert bits of their philosophy of life into their classes. Mabel demonstrated, usually by her own example, how with hard work, wit, and study, one could make a positive difference in the world. During a General Science course, B.E. gave us an explanation of Comunism which I have never forgotten. At that time the United States and the USSR were allies, and everyone was talking about the similarities between the two systems, Democracy and Communism. B.E. pointed out that in the United States, our constitution guaranteed that everyone was to have **equal opportunity**, and we must always protect that right. In the case of the USSR, everyone was to **be equal**, and not even the dictator, Stalin, would be able to make that so. He predicted that the USSR would fail eventually, because under the Communust system of government no one would have the incentive to try to excel.

I'm sure that each of their former students will judge the Trumps in his or her own way, but certainly Mabel's and B.E.'s traits of personality---their loyalty to the school, community, and country, their self confidence, their determination, their belief in the worth of each student, have stood out like roadsigns, and assisted each of us in plotting our way along life's highway.

THE HEALTHGIVERS
Part I

In the 30's, with money tight or non existant, there were a great many people who looked upon a visit to the doctor as an extravagance to be avoided if at all possible. Although immunization shots were urged for all youngsters, and a physician's attendance at the birth of a baby was highly desirable, there were some of my schoolmates who had never been to a doctor when they started to high school. Yet, in Plainview, I fear, we probably took good medical care for granted. Plainview always had doctors, since Dr. Edwin Lewis Taylor set up his practice in the city in 1880. Over the years various medical men had come and gone, and as a boy I heard people still talk about the legendary Dr. Kile, who had practiced medicine in Plainview from before the turn of the century until his death in 1912. But Plainview's doctors were not legends to me. They were my friends. Three medical doctors lived on North Main Street, my street; Dr. Nye, Dr. Jensen, and Dr. Melerian. Another, Dr. L.A. Johnson, lived just one block to the west. Dr. M.A. Johnson, who took Dr. L.A.'s place in Plainview, lived just around the corner. Both dentists, Dr. Fickling, and Dr. Ruzicka, lived within three houses of ours. In addition, the Plainview General Hospital was just across the intersection.

Collectively, these doctors were a fascinating group of medical men. Individually, they each had riveting stories to tell, about their early struggles to get an education, the early years of practice in Plainview, and the people they worked with along the way. In those Pre-Penicillin, Pre-Medical Insurance, Pre-WW II days, they took care of our medical needs with Experience, Common Sense, and Compassion.

Dr. Nye had come to Plainview in the 90's and practiced medicine in Plainview until his death in 1944. He said that in the early years he spent almost as much time extracting teeth and lancing abcesses as he did doing medical treatment. Early on he also mixed and dispensed medicines. During the flu epidemic of 1918 he regularly worked 18 and 20 hour days, from winter till late spring, tending the needs of the flu victims.

Dr. Nye delivered over 1000 babies during his career, most of them in the mother's home, and many of them with the assistance of Florence McMahon, "Plainview's Baby Nurse". He was instrumental in urging the use of deep wells rather than surface water in the communities of Foster and Plainview, showing the people that contaminated water was responsible for many deaths from typhoid and cholera.

During the 30's, Dr. Nye's grandson, Bill Nye, visited his grandparents, each summer from Omaha, and immediately became a part of the neighborhood scene. Occasionally he would take us upstairs in his grandparents' home to see the "old hospital". Before 1917 Dr. Nye used part of the second floor of his home as an operating room, and on the third floor there were beds for recovering patients. By the time we visited the rooms, they had not been used for hospital purposes for many years, and they were quite crowded with the equipment from the old hospital. It really was a grand place to play. We took turns lying on the beds while Bill, who insisted on being "doctor", since it was his grandfather's operating room, donned surgical gown and mask, and pretended to remove an appendix or brain tumor. There were other appliances available, and someone was always walking around on crutches with his leg in a splint, or his head swathed in bandages.

Dr. Nye had a farm on the way to the Country Club, and already before WW II he had built up an outstanding herd of Black Angus cattle, of which he was justifibly proud. He said that every man should have a hobby, and if that hobby happened to make money rather than costing money that was so much the better.

Mrs. Nye's hobby was writing poetry. On their farm was a grove of trees where she had built a little cabin, and during the summer days she would retreat to her little hideaway to read and contemplate nature, and then put her experience into verse.

Dr. Jensen was born in Denmark in 1871, and received his early education in Denmark. He graduated from the University of Nebraska Medical School in 1903, at which time he set up practice in Plainview. He was mostly retired when I knew him. He built wooden cabinets and furniture; he liked to putter in his garden, and he loved to visit. When the hospital had been in Dr. Nye's home, he had regularly administered anesthetic for the operations. Before WW I he served several years as County Physician. In the 30's he still saw patients, and was on the staff at the hospital.

But he seemed to long for the "old days". He had kept a cow in his back yard until the city passed an ordnance banning large animals within the city limits, and he still missed that cow. He told how, in years past, he had used a horse and buggy on his visits to the country to deliver babies. On the long ride home he was invariably

131

exhausted, and often the weather was bad. It didn't matter, though, because the horse knew the way, and he could drop the reins and sleep while the horse made his way home without guidance. He grumbled that he still got tired on the way home from visits to the country, and now, with his black Chevy coupe, when he dozed off, he found himself in the ditch and had to be pulled out by one of the farmers.

Dr. Melerian was born in Turkey, in 1868. He came to America in 1887, and set up medical practice in Brunswick in 1896. In 1917 he came to Plainview as the first administrator of the new Plainview Hospital. He served in that capacity for the first five years. During that time his wife, Mary (nee Johnson), helped by working in the kitchen, on the floor with patients, or wherever she was needed.

In 1922, Dr. Melerian resigned his post as hospital administrator and set up practice in a building one half block north of the bank on Main Street. His story was worthy of Horatio Alger. He had come to America with absolutely no money, but with an all consuming desire to succeed. He worked to learn the English language, then worked to put himself through Rush Medical College in Chicago. He said that his ambition, in the beginning, was to work long enough to own his home and have $8000 in the bank, which he deemed sufficient to retire. When he had attained that goal he decided that he needed to do more, so he bought a farm and proceeded to pay that off. When that goal was reached he set another and another. By the time WW II came along he finally decided that he was financially secure and retired from his practice, only to die in 1942. An absorbing account of his life is contained in his book, "My Fifty Four Years On American Shores".

Dr. L.A. Johnson was an Iowan who came to Plainview in 1915. He had a brother in Wausa who was also a doctor and the two brothers covered for one another, making vacations possible for both men. His first wife was a fine musician and played for many local social affairs as well as serving as pianist for the silent movies. Dr. L.A. was a good musician as well, and played the trombone in the town band for a number of years.

His office was next to the bakery, on the south side of Locust street, and he was a frequent visitor at the bakery. He was also a chess playing buddy of my father's, and they frequently closed the door in his office for a quiet game of chess in the afternoon.

One afternoon I was helping my Dad move some racks in the bakery and managed to jar loose a heavy steel pressure plate from the bread moulder, which hung on the end of the rack. When Dad moved the rack the pressure plate came loose and hit him across the end of his foot, nearly severing his big toe. I was in a near state of panic, but managed to go next door to summon Dr. Johnson. He was calm, and managed to calm me as well, and together we were able to help my Dad into the office where he proceeded to remove the shoe, clean the wound, and do the surgery necessary to save the toe.

The toe was saved, but the toe nail was badly crippled and ever after, that toe nail has had to be trimmed by a doctor. When the operation was over, Dr. Johnson laughed and told me that I should know that my Dad would always think of me when it was time to have that toe nail trimmed.

One time Dad and I were in Dr. L.A.'s office, I suppose on one of the toe nail trimming visits. Afterward, the two men stood at the front of the office, visiting as they gazed out onto the street. Dr. Johnson's wife had died a year or so before, of complications following a spinal operation, and he seemed particularly depressed. He said that business was pretty good, but no one had any money, and he wasn't sure how much longer he could exist on chickens and vegetables that people brought in to pay off their medical bills. While they talked he twice called attention to a a child going by on the street, saying, "That kid still is not paid for", and "That boy was paid for by one chicken and an apple pie".

In 1938, three years after his first wife had died, Dr. Johnson married Ruth Hoffman, the widow of John Hoffman, the theater owner. Soon after that the Johnsons left Plainview and Dr. Johnson assumed a position as a government doctor for the C.C.C. camps. In 1941 he settled in Norfolk, where he served as staff physician at the Norfolk State Hospital, until his retirement in 1965.

Dr. M.A. Johnson, from Wausa, graduated from the University of Nebraska Medical school in 1936, and for a time served as Camp Surgeon in a Missouri C.C.C. camp. In 1937 he located his practice of medicine in Plainview and served the community in that capacity until his death in 1959. During his tenure in Plainview he was instrumental in attaining a major addition to the hospital in 1950, as well as the construction of a new doctors' clinic in 1952.

Dr. M.A. Johnson was a friend of my dad's and I remember him, in the early years, as someone who liked to have a good time. He was a good ping pong player and some of the tournaments that took place in our basement got to be very spirited. He also delivered our second daughter in 1955 and insisted that I be a delivery room observer of the birth, if not an active assistant. The coffee and conversation he offered me when the event was over allowed my shaking knees to recover enough so that I could drive home.

But the event that sticks in my mind when I think of Dr. M.A. is one that happened during the war. Whereas during the 30's Plainview had almost a surplus of doctors, by the time the war came along, suddenly there was a shortage. Dr. Nye, Dr. Melerian, and Dr. Jensen were old and semi-retired, and all the young doctors were being called to the service. Dr. M.A. Johnson was handling the entire medical burden of the Plainview vicinity, almost single handedly, and continued to do so until he was joined by Dr. Kopp in 1948. Where before he laughed easily and always had a quip or a story, now he was mostly quiet and always looked haggard.

I must have been a junior in high school, and a carload of us had been to a dance at the West Randolph Ballroom. It was long after midnight when we got back to Plainview. There was no traffic on the streets until we got to the library corner. Then, suddenly, a car crossed the highway immediately in front of us. The driver was going too fast and lost control of his vehicle and slammed into the light pole in front of the library, almost shearing the pole from its base.

When we got to the car the driver was slumped over the steering wheel and blood was streaming down the side of his face. The others in our group tried to help the stricken driver while I ran to the telephone office

135

down the street and called Dr. Johnson. He answered on the third ring and told us that we should keep the driver still and he would be down directly.

When Dr. Johnson got to the accident scene five minutes later, I was sorry that we had called. He looked as if it were he that should be going to the hospital. He had been on duty with surgery and other emergencies for more than 24 hours and had just gotten to bed. His face was drawn and grey and his shoulders sagged. And when he saw the driver he let out a little oath. "Damn you, Frederick, one of these times your're going to break your fool neck!" It turned out that Frederick was the drunken driver and this was the third time that Dr. Johnson had pulled him out of a wreck that year. Frederick was unhurt, other than a superficial cut on his forehead, and was soon revived, but was still in a very relaxed state. We offered to take him home, but Dr. Johnson said that he knew where he lived and would take him home and explain to his wife what had happened. He assured us that we had done right to call him, but we never-the-less felt much guilt over our part in depriving him of his badly needed sleep.

THE HEALTHGIVERS
Part II

Dr. Fickling and Dr. Ruzicka had offices in second story locations on opposite corners of the main intersection in downtown Plainview. They also lived just around the corner from one another in my neighborhood. Dr. Fickling was a rather tall man, with an unusually long, loping stride. Dr. Ruzicka, on the other hand, was just over five feet tall, and took very short, quick steps. Morning, noon, and night, these two friends, like Mutt and Jeff, walked together to and from work, engaged in deep conversation, to the point that they would fail to acknowledge neighbors as they passed.

Dr. Fickling had made a honeymoon trip to Alaska, by ship, years before and gave very descriptive accounts of the icebergs and whales that he had seen on that trip. As a member of the library board he was responsible for numerous books on travel and adventure in the library. For his office waiting room he subscribed to "True Detective" and other detective magazines. My mother was a detective story fan, and she would always bring several of these magazines home with her after her visit to the dentist. She and Dr. Fickling would argue the merits of the detective process that one or another of the sleuths had used in solving his case.

Dr. Fickling, from rural Yankton, South Dakota, came to Plainview in 1909, after graduating from Creighton U. Dental School. He was a great sportsman. He looked forward to pheasant hunting season and hunted ducks in the lakes around Valentine. He was also a baseball fan, and if you happened to have your appointment during the World Series you could be sure that the radio, low in the background, would be tuned to the game of the day.

Dr. Fickling and his wife, Nell, were both enthusiastic golfers. They were charter members of the Country Club, and were instrumental in organizing golf tournaments at the local golf course. Nell thought that all of the neighborhood children should learn to play golf, and repeatedly offered to teach us herself. We resisted. Why, I can't imagine, but the truth is that most of us did not learn golf's basics until we were grown and gone from Plainview.

Dr. Ruzicka was born in Wilbur, Nebraska and after graduating from the University of Nebraska Dental College, set up his practice in Plainview in 1915. He was very active in civic affairs; Lions Club, The Country Club, The Chamber of Commerce, The Masonic Lodge, and the Library Board, as well various Dental organizations.

Dr. and Mrs. Ruzicka loved to travel. When their son, Bob, who had been one of my early heroes, moved to California, they got plenty of opportunities to see the country. Dr. Joe treated these long trips with much the same enthusiasm that he put into everything else he did. For years they made the trip to California to see Bob and his family once or twice a year. Instead of taking the same road each time, which he felt would be boring, they tried to take a different route each time. On one occasion he announced that he thought he could lead tours to the far west, and he would be able to point out the shortest route, the most scenic, the flattest, or any other criteria you could name. He'd driven them all.

Dr. Ruzicka played baseball for many years on the Plainview town team, and it was said that those short legs were a blur in beating a throw to first base. But during the years I knew him, Joe Ruzicka was best known for his music. He was a charter member of the Plainview Town Band in 1923; served as its assistant director and announcer. He played bass tuba in that band, and in the subsequent Klown Band until his death in 1968. He also was choir director at the Congregational Church for many many years, and often the only bass singer in the choir. He had a rich bass voice, and his solo in the Anthem, "He Arose" was a traditional treat on Easter

Morn. For many, he was known as "The Little Man With The Big Bass Horn and Big Bass Voice".

Dr. Alfred Axford was a jeweler, watch maker, and optometrist. He had grown up west of Plainview, attended Plainview Normal College, and graduated from the Northwestern School of Optometry in Chicago. After taking out a land claim and working for some years in Pierre, South Dakota, he established his office in Plainview in 1917.

Dr. Alf and I had something in common that we both thought was significant. Our fathers both were bakers. His father though, had been a baker in the British Royal Navy, and he told me about the bad working conditions aboard ship, which resulted in his father's coming down with tuberculosis. When the doctor advised clean air, he left the Her Majesty's Navy and eventually settled in the wide open spaces of Antelope County Nebraska, where Alf was born.

Dr. Axford's office was on the north side of Locust St., and only occupied one half of the building. His two daughters had a beauty parlor business in the other half. Being fitted for glasses in that office was an experience. Dr. Axford didn't have the modern optometrist's equipment, and instead, the patient put on a pair of oversized spectacles, into which he would insert corrective lenses, one after another, until the proper correction was achieved. My glasses always required a great deal of correction, so that by the time the examination was finished the spectacles were so heavy that I could scarcely hold my head up.

Dr. Axford had worked out an interesting retirement plan. Early on in his career, as soon as he could afford it, he began to buy up houses in Plainview, which he would rent out. His object was to have all of the houses paid off by the time he retired, and the rent from the houses would support him from then on. It was a good plan and he did accumulate a number of houses, but in the 30's rents were very low, and Dr. Axford was very good to people who got behind in their rent, so it is questionable just how well his plan turned out.

The Plainview General Hospital, originally a ten bed institution, was built in 1917. When Dr. Melerian left as administrator in 1923, Miss Etta Falconer assumed the duties of Superintendent of the Hospital, which included Head Nurse, General Manager, and Bookkeeper.

In those early, depression days, when corn was selling for ten cent per bushel, the hospital personnel had a variety of duties. When hospital bills were paid with vegetables or meat the staff canned this food for patients' use. The nurses washed out laundry at night, and hung it outdoors or in the basement in the morning. They also tended a large garden, and during Miss Falconer's tenure the hospital was noted for its fine garden.

Miss Falconer assisted Dr. L.A. Johnson in my sister's birth in 1931. I always found her a rather stern figure, but she followed my sister's progress through the years with great satisfaction, and the two of them remained good friends during the years they both lived in Plainview. In 1935 Miss Falconer retired from the hospital. She and George Dufek, a prominent retired Eden Valley farmer and widower, were married and they moved to his large home on east Locust Street.

Nellie McMahon Foft and her sister, Florence McMahon were synonymous with the hospital during the time I was growing up. Nellie joined the hopital staff in 1932, assumed the title of Nursing Director in 1937, and served in that capacity until her retirement in 1950. During much of this time she was assisted by her sister.

Nellie and Florence lived at the hospital, and so did Nellie's son, Billy. Billy and I were in the same class in school, and spent a great deal of time together, either at our house, or at his, which was the hospital. At the time this did not seem at all strange to me. Billy was good company. The hospital was a great place to visit, and I loved being asked to stay for dinner. Billy's Aunt Florence was really a lot of fun. She had a dry humor and was a very good cook.

It must have been difficult for Nellie, being on constant call, to provide a semblance of a normal home life, but she did a very good job of it. Billy told of emergencies during the night, at which time his mother and Aunt would have to get up to assist in a baby delivery or an operation and often would get no more sleep that night. But Nellie was invariably cordial to me, and was interested in what Billy and I were doing in school, and always concerned that we were doing "what was right".

One summer there was a very serious auto accident just west of town. At least one person was killed, and Rachel, a girl a little older than we were, was brought to the hospital with broken bones, and internal injuries. Dr. L.A. Johnson, I believe, was the attending physician, and for the next few days Dr. Johnson, or Nellie or Florence were with her constantly, round the clock. They literally nursed her through her crisis.

Once she was out of danger, Rachel's mother left Plainview to be with the rest of her family, in Ohio, and had to leave her daughter behind in Plainview to mend enough till she could travel. For the next two or three weeks Billy and I visited Rachel every day. We played cards and checkers and worked a lot with maps. She showed us where the family had been on vacation and where she lived in Ohio, and we showed her things about Nebraska, and Billy lectured to us both about how it was in Arizona and Wyoming, both places where he had lived. Toward the end of her stay Nellie and Florence arranged a little "going away party". They took Rachel outside and we had a picnic on the lawn. The neighborhood gang came over for cake and ice cream and we all celebrated Rachel's recovery. It was a sad day for us when her family came to drive her home. We were happy that she was going to fully recover her health of course, but we knew we were losing a friend that we would probably never see again.

I feel privileged that during the years I was growing up in Plainview I had occasion to know some of the pioneers in Plainview's medical community. Those dedicated men and women, using the tools and technology available, looked after our medical needs the best way they knew how, always striving to do more for their patient. In doing so they laid the foundation for the fine medical facilities, tradition, and personnel that Plainview enjoys today.

CITY SERVICES I

During a planning meeting for an air raid drill during WWII, E.G. Dickinson, the overall director of the Civil Defense Committee reminded the volunteers that Plainview's Light Plant was the very heart of of our town, and it was of utmost importance to protect that building and keep the generators producing electricity for the city. Throughout the war we were reminded that Plainview was fortunate, in that if large power sources were destroyed in the United States, Plainview would still be able to function because we had our own power plant.

These were no doubt grandiose statements concerning our source of power, but they do underscore the pride that people in Plainview felt for their very own power supply. But like a good many issues in Plainview over the years, a power plant did not come without a good bit of argument. As late as the turn of the century Plainview's citizens could not even decide on the power source for street lights, gas or electricity.

Finally the issue was settled and the first power station was built in Plainview in 1901. Charles Axford was the manager. That first steam powered generator enabled the business places and the homes in Plainview to be hooked up to electricity. Later some farms north of the city were hooked up , and eventually the city entered into an agreement with the Eden Valley farmers to supply them with electricity as well, though most of the farms around Plainview had to wait till the end of WWII for the REA to provide them with electricity. At first electricity was only provided in the evenings for lights. Anyone wishing to have lights for a party was charged $1 per hour after midnight. An exception to the daytime ban of electricity came on Monday and Tuesday mornings, washing and ironing days.

Over the years a number of generators were purchased, each larger and more expensive than the last. The first diesel powered generator was bought in 1929 for $27,580. The last one cost $172,500, in 1957. At that time it was reported that "The municipal light plant now has adequate power for all purposes at all times". But with the post war explosion in the demand for electricity, as air conditioners and other appliances came into being, it was eventually decided, with reluctance, that it would be prudent to buy electricity from outside sources and only use the local system as a backup in the case of emergency.

At the bakery we frequently needed to pick up ice in the middle of the night. The ice house was located in the light plant building, and we needed to have the power generator operator help us as he was the only one on duty. Invariably we would find him in the generator room, fast asleep on a little cot next to his huge generator. The noise in that room was deafening. Shouting to him was of no use at all, and we would have to shake him to get him awake. We used to joke about the cushy job that he had, only making routine inspections a few times a night and sleeping the rest of time. Then one night I was at the light plant to pick up ice. I had just gone into the generator room to shake the operator awake when the drone of the generator changed, dropped in pitch the least bit. Instantly, the operator was on his feet, wide awake, scurrying to ascertain the cause of the trouble. That little change in the sound of the generator, signaling either low or high voltage, had instantly alerted him to trouble. I decided there and then, that despite appearances, he indeed was ready at all times to do what was necessary to keep that generator operating properly.

In the early days of this century Plainview's ice came in large blocks, cut from the frozen rivers and shipped into the city in insulated railroad cars. It was then stored in an ice house adjacent to the depot where, covered with straw, it lasted throughout the summer.

From 1919 on, the City manufactured it own "pure and good tasting" ice in a room next to the jail, in the Light Plant building. The water was frozen in 300 pound blocks, which were immediately broken down into manageable 100 pound blocks. Later these big blocks were broken down into 50 and 25 pound units for the retail trade. It was incredible how with just a few swipes of the ice pick a skilled worker could break the large block into designated sizes, exactly straight across, with very little waste.

And yes, early on, Plainview did have an ice man, who would "commeth" to your house three times per week and leave ice in your "ice box", the amount determined by the little card that you left in your front window. In the early days the ice wagon was horse drawn, the horse stopping, automatically, at each home. In the summer the ice wagon was popular with the neighborhood children who followed along and picked up the ice chips, sort of a forerunner of the Good Humor Ice Cream Man.

By the mid 30's most of the homes had electric "ice boxes" and the delivery of ice was terminated, but the City continued to make its own ice until 1959. The bakery was a big user of ice, especially in the summer.

We used it to cool the doughs as they mixed in the large horizontal bread mixer. Toward the end the ice making machinery seemed to need almost constant repair. I'm sure that my Dad's pleas to the council to keep the machinery going were largely instrumental in the decision to continue in the ice making business as long as they did

My folks were always very pleased with Plainview's water. They said that it was the best tasting water anywhere. They were probably easy to please as they came from Presho, in the west river country of South Dakota, where water was scarce. The wells were artesian, and the water in the taps was warm and filled with so many minerals that it stained all the fixtures a reddish yellow, and until an individual got used to drinking that water, it made one extremely sick with stomach cramps.

Until after the turn of the century, in Plainview, individual and neighborhood wells provided the community's water. In 1898, P.D. Corell built a "large tower surmounted by a windmill and containing a large tank sufficiently elevated to carry water to all parts of his residence and lawn with considerable force."-PV News.

The first City well and water system was put down in 1903. It hooked up residences and businesses to water, in addition to 15 hydrants, for fire control. However, it was not until 1923 that a sewage project was initiated. This 20 year gap between the two events seems strange today. However, even at that late date, 1923, it took considerable salesmanship to convince a number of the prominent families in Plainview that it was OK to bring the outhouse functions inside the home.

CITY SERVICES II

With the installation of the water system in town came interest in organized fire protection, and in 1903 the Plainview Volunteer Fireman's Association was formed. This, incidently, was also the year of the first Firemen's Ball. That first year the firemen's ball was held upstairs in the old Opera House. It evidently was a rousing affair, for in the minutes of the first meeting following the event, four men were dropped from membership in the organization, presumably for anti-social behavior at the ball. The first fire call was made in February, 1904, to the residence of N.P. Jeppesen, a call which the new fire department reportedly handled with great dispatch.

In the early years the Fire Chief was elected for a one year term, but beginning in 1915 Ernest (Dutch) Gast was elected Chief, a position he held for the next 47 years. For a number of years Dutch Gast and Alex Melchoir, of Wisner, were honored at firemen's meetings as the two Chiefs with the longest tenure in the state. (It should be added that during the latter years of that reign Dutch was able to continue because of the able assistance of Assistant Chief, Louis Petersen).

Dutch worked, for his livelihood, at Ebinger Hardware where his brother, Bill, was manager. He was as accomodating clerk as you ever find. Ebinger's was an old fashioned store that sold almost everything--hardware, plumbing, sheet metal, sporting goods, etc. (From the Plainview Republican, 1910---F.W. Ebinger: I sell the genuine Round Oak stoves, ranges, base burners and furnaces, the best on earth!) Ebinger's had merchandise stacked on shelves to the high ceiling. This required a tall ladder connected to a track in the ceiling and wheels on the floor, for the retrieval of merchandise on the high shelves. When I was quite small, Dutch would sometimes let me climb to near the top of the ladder, then push me, on the ladder, from one end of the store to the other. Dutch was also a baseball fan, and prided himself on the fact that he always presented the town team with a new ball at the beginning of each season.

Dutch Gast was a fixture in Plainview. He was a lifelong bachelor, although it was said that he was married to his one "love", the Fire Department, all his adult life. He missed only one Firemen's Meeting, City Council Meeting, or fire, during his time as Chief, a time when he was called to Omaha for jury duty. It was said that he lived and breathed fires 24 hours a day. He regularly carried a short length of fire hose with a coupling attached, and would practice attaching the hose to a hydrant on his way to work, to improve his time and technique. When he heard the fire whistle he would drop whatever he was doing to rush to the fire station. If he happened to be at the store, counting out your change when the fire whistle blew, he would throw the money on the counter and literally run out the door. It was said that he had memorized the layouts of all the buildings in downtown--the number of steps, arrangement of roms, etc., toward the time that he might have to find his way through those buildings in the dark or blinded by smoke.

During his time in office he saw the department grow from a collection of shovels and buckets, 1000 feet of hoses on two hand drawn carts, and a few waterproof coats, housed in a shed in back of the light plant, to one of fully equipped motorized fire trucks, housed in a modern fire station. Although Dutch was influential in the purchase of the first motorized fire truck in 1925, he never learned to drive that truck, or any other of the department's vehicles. In fact, he never did have a driver's license.

Though Dutch loved to visit, his conversation tended to be one dimensional. No matter what you started to talk about he would work it around to one of the fires in Plainview's past that he had fought. Especially memorable for him were:

1. Joe Henken's wooden department store on Locust Street in 1907.
2. The Methodist Church and Parsonage, 1909.
3. McHenry Mill, 1939, which began on the night of the Firemen's Ball while the firemen were celebrating at the Lakeview Ballroom, north of Brunswick.

He could recall every detail of these disasters and every other fire that had occurred in Plainview, and was only too happy to enlighten anyone he was talking to about them.

Dutch Gast, his brother Gus, and their maiden sister, Hattie, lived with their mother in a little house south and east of the firehouse, until Gus married, late in life, and moved with his bride to a house of their own. After their mother died Hattie continued to keep house for Dutch as long as I lived in Plainview.

Mother Gast was quite a small woman, but one with a great deal of grit. One story they told of her: In the south part of town, where they lived, the land was low, and it had been known to flood. On this occasion there was a tremendous rain and the water did come up around

149

the Gast dwelling. Mrs. Gast was home alone, as both boys were out with the firemen protecting property elsewhere, and Hattie was away visiting friends. When the water started to come in under the door Mrs. Gast, by herself, managed to get her prized pianola (a large record player) off the floor and onto two chairs, away from the water. When the water receded it was all the two boys, together, could do to get the pianola off the chairs and back into its proper place. Mrs. Gast had no recollection as to how she had managed the feat. She just remembered wanting to protect her record machine.

In the early days of Plainview, law enforcement was rather informal. One of the city workers would be assigned the task of fire watcher and door checker at night, for extra pay. For a long time the only system that was used to summon a policeman was to turn on a light atop the light plant which alerted the officer to trouble. Police trouble, through the 30's, seemed to consist mainly of drunkenness and disorderly conduct, and the small jail, located on the south side of the light plant building, was primarily used as a "sleep it off" facility.

Though the police force expanded during the 30's, the idea of a night watchman, whose duty it was to watch for fires and check doors, remained through the time, in 1957, that we left Plainview to come to McCook. At that time, between his rounds of checking doors, the night "Cop" regularly used a comfortable barber's chair in one of the two barbershops on Locust Street as his headquarters. From there he could observe the activity going on in downtown Plainview.

One night Gene Young and I had a slight "fender bender" on the street, right in front of the Loring Jenkin's barber shop, next to Baber's Cafe. It was not a serious

150

accident and Gene and I made arrangements on the spot to notify our insurance agents. Gene had already driven off, and I was about to leave, when the "Officer of the Law" came out of the barbershp and walked up to me. I started to tell him about the accident, but he interrupted me to say that he had seen the whole thing. He had been sitting in the darkened building, and I had not noticed him. He said that Gene and I seemed to be handling everything well, and if we took care of things ourselves it would save his having to file an accident report. A very civilized procedure in that civilized time and place.

WORLD WAR II
IN PLAINVIEW

From the Plainview News: It was a year ago or more that a little girl asked her grandfather to "tell her some stories about when he was a little boy."

That story-telling resulted in reminiscing, and eventually the reminiscences were put down on paper--and submitted to this newspaper because the reminiscences were in the Plainview of yesteryear...It is started now, prior to Memorial Day, 1992.

THOSE WAR YEARS IN PLAINVIEW

"Tell me about the war, Grandpa!". This is a request that senior citizens get a lot these days. The American people, kids included, have watched an entire war (the Persian Gulf War) during the time that I spent on one vacation trip to Texas this winter. And of course, that familiarity with how a war is fought and won has provoked interest in our country's other wars.

Since the Gulf War of 1991 there has been a great deal of discussion concerning the attitude of the American citizens toward the war, and contrasting the present attitude of the American people toward the other wars in our nation's history.

A good deal has been written about the overt signs of patriotism shown by the folks at home and how very different this was from the way the public responded to the Vietnam war, when servicemen were reluctant to wear their uniforms off the base. This current bit of flagwaving is a very refreshing change to be sure.

I had the opportunity to serve in the Army in Korea, and for the life of me, I really do not remember very much about the attitude of the home folks toward me. My family members were proud of me I'm sure, and were happy to have me home, and I really do not have any bad memories of my homecoming. Korea was really an extension of World War II, and everyone was mighty glad to have it over, including me; and I was so pleased to be mustered out of the Army that I did not take time to dwell on how I was treated. Certainly there were no parades awaiting our return, but then we didn't expect any either.

What I do remember, though, very clearly, was what went on in Plainview during World War II. I was 13 years old, and in the eighth grade when the war began. Mrs. Chase, the principal of the Junior High, and our history teacher, was concerned that we know what was going on in the world around us, as well as the world of English, Math, and Science. So our class was pretty current about the events leading up to the outbreak of war.

The scene in Plainview was probably repeated many times in small towns across the land. Plainview, I'm sure, was quite a typical small town, and yet in one respect Plainview was unusual--in the great number of young men from the community who died in the war. By the 1940 census, Plainview had a population of 1411. According to the Plainview Memorial Day program, 26 Plainview boys have lost their lives serving our country, all but four in WWII. Surely Plainview has paid a horrible price in the blood of its young men shed during that war.

Like everyone my age and older, I remember distinctly where I was when I heard the news that the Japanese had bombed Pearl Harbor. That Sunday afternoon had been balmly, for early December, and we had just come out of a matinee performance of "Navy Blues", starring Jack Oakie and Martha Raye, a light hearted tale of life in the peacetime Navy, at the Plains Theater. Kenny Dickinson announce the news to us as we came outside, and then we had a big discussion as to just where Pearl Harbor was, and what this would all mean. At home we listened on the radio till late into the night for further war developments.

Next morning the whole school, grades as well a high school, were herded into the high school gym to hear President Roosevelt's famous "This Day Will Live In Infamy" address to the nation, in which he declared war on Germany as well as Japan.

I did not have a brother or close relative that was in the service, but the war went on for so long, for 3 1/2 years, my entire high school career, that we were all touched by it in so many ways.

Boys had been drafted even before Pearl Harbor, of course, and Leo Armstrong, the brother of one of my classmates had gone to Canada, volunteering to fight with the RCAF. In the beginning there was a little send-off for the boys when they went off to service, but after December 7th, it seemed that someone was leaving for the service all the time. Soon we began to get reports that some of these boys were killed or missing in action. And in a small town those were not just names in the newpaper, but guys I knew, or at least I knew their families, and some were personal friends and heroes of mine.

Bob Couchman and I were both members of Mr. George's town band. If Norman Rockwell had been looking for a model of the "All American Boy" he might well have picked Bob, with his red hair and freckles, and devilish grin. He was a great tease, and a favorite with the younger guys in the band. He played the slide

155

trombone well, and with great enthusiasm. One of the treats at a Friday night summer band concert was to play "Lassus Trombone", or "Hold That Tiger", or another of the trombone numbers, featuring Bob Couchman on the trombone. He really hammed it up, and these numbers were as much fun for the band members as they were for the audience. Bob was an early casualty of the war. I remember that Mr. George announced Bob's death at a Monday night band rehersal, and a bit later talked about him and his music. Then we played "Lassus Trombone" in his memory, but no one could play the trombone part like Bob could, and the tribute fell a little flat.

Gene Hecht was a little older than I, but he was not a very large boy, and he lived not too far from our house. Sometimes he would look in on our games in the park, and would occasionally umpire. One day he was riding his bike up town, showing off for a girl, I think. Anyway, he was riding without using his hands, and going in circles in the intersection by the bank. All of a sudden a car came around the corner and Gene ran right into it. I thought sure that he had killed himself, and I was among a group of people who ran out to pull him and his bike out from under the car. He was dazed, and had the largest bump on his head. His bike had a sprung frame, and two badly twisted wheels, but otherwise he was okay. Soon after that he went into the Air Force.

Sometime later I was again at the bank intersection when we spotted an Air Force plane approaching. It was flying low, so low in fact, that it looked like it was going to crash, right into the Main Street intersection. It was really a fascinating sight, that big plane, a B-17 Flying Fortress, I think, flying so low that the wing tips looked as if they would hit the

156

buildings on either side of the street. The noise was so loud that you could not possibly hear anyone speak, or scream, though I'm sure that people were doing both. It was confusing, and had we not seen the stars on the wings I'm sure we would have thought that the enemy was upon us.

That first pass came on us so quickly we really did have a chance to think about it, but fortunately the pilot gave us another look. In a matter of moments, back he came again, if anything even lower this time. I could only stand where I was and stare. The plane was so low that you could very clearly see faces in the windows, and in the side turret window there was a fellow waving for all he was worth. Now I can't say that I could recognize anyone going by me that fast, no matter how low he was, but I can say that when we heard some days later that it had been Gene Hecht's plane that had buzzed Plainview on the way to England, I was not at all suprised. But that was the last that Plainview saw of Gene. He was killed on a bombing mission later over Germany later that year.

Don Bivens was the eldest of three athletic brothers. I don't remember that he excelled at team sports, but he was tough as nails, and a great competitor. Once, at a school picnic south of town, we both jumped for a forward pass and collided, heads first. Don was apparently not hurt, but I had a knot over my eye as large as an egg, and couldn't open that eye for a week.

Perhaps I was lucky to realize how tough Don was without challenging him, because later Don was entered in a boxing program at school. He was matched with a much larger boy, and it looked as if it was going to be a mismatch. It was, but not in the way that everyone had supposed. Don came out like a whirlwind, a flurry of

157

arms and legs, with no boxing style at all. It really didn't matter though, because he threw so many punches that the other boy was never able to counter. The fight was called, and Don won, by a TKO.

This fierce competitive spirit was the thing that drove him to want to be in the army I suppose, but I remember that his concern was that the war would be over before he could get there. He left for the army before he finished high school. The war did last long enough for him to get there. He was one of the war's last casualties from Plainview.

Early on, during the war there was a directive that each town should have a civil defense program. Plainview complied, with gusto. There was a series of meetings at the library, and a team was selected to care for Plainview in event of a catastrophe. The catastrophe could be of any nature, but at that time the only catastrophe that anyone thought about was an attack by enemy planes.

E.G. Dickinson was appointed the Civil Defense chairman, and I remember that my Dad was an air raid warden, the theory being, I guess, that since he worked at the bakery at night he might be the one to spot the enemy planes and sound the alarm. Anyway, in due course, a plan of action was set in place and instructions to the populace published, and a mock air raid planned.

As a kid I thought that it was all great fun. I had been appointed to an important job. I was a messenger, along with Alice Dickinson, one of my classmates. We were assigned to Chairman Dickinson's house, which was the main headquarters. Our job was to be ready to run to the various posts with instructions in case the telephones were knocked out.

The air raid signal sounded (the town fire whistle, naturally), and the emergency was upon us. This must have been January, or February, 1942, as it was dark early in the evening. We hurried to our posts, and for awhile we did practice taking a few messages to one or another of the wardens, and then walking with the wardens on their rounds.

The wardens all had flashlights covered with some kind of blue cloth, which supposedly made the beam invisible to enemy aircraft. The only bit of uniform they had was a white arm band, their badge of authority. Their duty, on their rounds, was to see that all of the residents either had all lights off, or had their windows covered tightly. Generally people cooperated very well, but occasionally a warden would have to use his authority and explain how any little light, even a lighted cigarette coule be seen from thousands of feet in the air, and from many miles. He could also threaten police action.

After a time we tired of walking around neighborhoods in the dark and went back to the Dickinson headquarters. The windows of the house were blacked out in the prescribed manner, but additionally the house was mostly dark, and the men pored over their maps and orders at the dining room table, which was lighted by just one small lamp. This was much better than being outside. The telephone system was working fine. Mrs. Dickinson had a plate of cookies, and Alice and I sat on the radiator at the fringes of light and held hands while the grown-ups played war.

After that first year, when there were no real or imagined air raids, someone must have pointed out that if Plainview, pop. 1411, in almost the exact center of the United States were to be attacked by enemy aircraft the

United States was probably in deep trouble. Anyway, even though the machinery was in place, just in case, we didn't spend much time during the rest of the war worrying about an enemy attack on Plainview.

At school we spent a great deal of time emulating the men in service. Each boy had his favorite branch of service and really looked upon the other brances as a bit inferior. Each girl in school had at least one serviceman to whom whe was writing. And the girls talked endlessly about the G.I mail they had received. I'm sure that we boys were jealous of all this. We took pains to look like G.I.'s. A G.I. haircut was the standard trim. Khaki pants and shirts were the school clothes of choice. We walked and talked like G.I.'s, or at least how the movies portrayed G.I.'s.

This led to one practice that I didn't start, but I'm afraid that I helped bring to a screeching halt. One of the boys in high school got a set of Private 1st Class stripes from his brother in the Army and decided to sew these stripes on his khaki shirt, just like a real soldier. Soon after another boy sewed corporal stripes on his shirt, and before long almost everyone had stripes on his shirt, and the stripes began to become more numerous. One boy was going around as a Master Sergeant.

This bit of one-upmanship was too good to pass up, so one night I cut up a tin can into little rectangles, which I fastened to my khaki shirt, and immediately became Plainview High's only 1st Lieutenant.

That was too much for B.E.Trump, acting for the administration, and during first period all of us who had stripes or bars on our shirts were summoned to the office and summarily ordered to get everything off our shirts and quit impersonating a serviceman.

160

B.E.Trump had been in the Army during World War I, but as far a I was concerned, he and his wife, Mabel, had been in the Plainview school system since the beginning of time. When I first knew him he was teaching manual training, and apparently was very happy doing just that. But the war called for heroic measures, and as teachers left for the service B.E. was called upon to fill a variety of positions. At one time or another he taught most high school subjects, plus he handled the duties of Principal, Superintendent, and Coach.

B.E. was handling the duties of basketball coach when an incident occurred which has stuck in my mind. He must have been the assistant coach, because he seemed to be working mostly with us younger players.

His uniform on the court was the same one that he wore all the time, dark suit pants, shirt and tie, but instead of a suit coat he wore a very heavy red coat sweater. He didn't even change out of his street shoes when he took to the basketball court. It really didn't matter because he didn't move around on the court that much anyway.

One of his first teaching assignments had been in Iowa, where he inherited the position of coach. He had never played basketball, but had read a book on the subject. Nevertheless, his team suprised many people as the year wore on. The boys had knocked off teams from much larger schools enroute to a berth in the state championship game. It seems that their secret was to work the ball around till the other team got dizzy watching so many passes, then go in for an easy basket. So for the entire practice session we would practice weaving in and out, constantly passing the ball, at least 20 times before taking a shot at the basket. This was not

161

too much fun, and we all doubted the wisdom of such practice, but B.E. assured us that it would pay off for us.

Natuarally, there was quite a bit of griping over our not being allowed to shoot, and one day one of the players made the comment that B.E. must not even know what a set shot was.(In those days we all took two-handed set shots, as a one-handed jump shot was considered being out of control.) He was good natured about the remark, and countered with the claim that he not only knew what a set shot was, but as a player he had been able to sink baskets from the center of the court, not only facing the basket, but backwards, over his head. This remark provoked not a few groans and jeers. He listened for just a moment, then picked up two basketballs and walked to the circle at the center of the court. He set one basketball on the floor, looked over his shoulder at the basket, then squared up, and using two hands, tossed the ball over his head, and swished the ball through the hoop. Then, without waiting, he picked up the other ball, turned around a tossed the ball over his head toward the other basket. This time it did not swish, but banked off the backboard, and dropped through the basket.

There was not a sound as B.E. turned and walked off the court. He didn't say a word or crack a smile. We were stunned. Granted, our court was not full sized, but it was an example of shooting that I've never seen duplicated. I never saw B.E. pick up a basketball again.

Playing an inter-school sports schedule during the war was very difficult. Besides having coaches drafted and leaving, there was the matter of getting transportation to the out-of-town games. Gas and tires were rationed, so there was always a scramble as game day approaced, to line up enough cars in the community to get the team to the game. Farm boys were invaluable in this regard. While most of the people in town had "A" type cards, farmers had "B" or "C", and could usually be counted on for the extra gas or an occasional tire.

But Plainview's secret weapon in that regard had to be Bob Bush. Bob was a little round man. He wore thick glasses which were tinted pink, and when he talked to you he blinked a lot. He was always chewing gum, but this did not stop him from also smoking big cigars. He had come to Plainview before the war and had prospered in an insurance and real estate business, and later an automobile and implement business. He knew everyone, and he enjoyed his reputation as a wheeler-dealer.

Bob loved sports, and the rumor was that he made large bets on the game. At any rate, he was on hand for all the games, at home or away, and could be counted on to arrange transportation if that should be a problem. Both his businesses brought him into contact with many farmers, and we speculated that he was able to swap goods and services for extra ration cards.

Going to away games required extra time on the road, as the speed limit was only 35 miles per hour. It was hard to hold the speed to 35, especially if you got a late start, which Bob invariably did. In those wartime days if you did pass a car, going over the speed limit, the driver of the other car would honk his horn and give you the two finger, V for Victory sign, letting you know that you were not doing your part in furthering the war effort.

Going 35 miles per hour was not conducive to Bob's flamboyant nature at any time, and certainly not when he was on his way to a game, so when these honks came his way he cheerfully waved and honked back, three short blasts, and one long blast, the international morse code symbol for V, and the audible counterpart to the two fingered "V for Victory" salute.

On the way to the games Bob would announce that if the team won he'd buy us lunch after the game. I know we didn't always win, but I don't remember ever going home hungry.

Besides gas and tires, sugar, butter and lard were also rationed. When rationing first began, my mother decided to make us all aware of just how little butter we would be allowed. She divided the family butter ration for the week into four equal portions and placed them on the little doll dishes that my sister had. At each meal she would place our individual plate of butter before us. This really had a strong effect on our appetites, and we would shave a very thin slice of butter for our bread. The result was that at the end of the week we each had at least half of our alloted ration left. Apparently that was all the lesson we needed, because after that the butter supply for the family was again placed on one plate, and I never heard about not having enough butter again.

Sugar was in short supply, and though my mother had to cut down on the amount of home canning she was able to do, we never did run out of sugar at home. (Since we had the bakery, my mother did no baking at home. That helped lots.)

Sugar at the bakery was another matter. Because people wanted to conserve on sugar at home they bought lots of cake and pastries at the bakery. The bakery had a sugar allowance, of course, but business was very good--so good that twice during the war my Dad had to close the bakery, for a week each time, until his next sugar ration was available. And one time, when he was trying to stretch the sugar supply, and had stopped baking cakes, a lady brought him extra sugar ration stamps so that he could bake her daughter's wedding cake.

By the end of the war everything was in short supply. Cars and farm vehicles were worn out, but new ones were simply not available. My Dad had always bought a new car every other year from the time he came to Plainview, but his '41 Chevy, bought in late 1940 had to last until 1946 when the supply of new cars once more was ample. There was always the rumor that if you were willing to pay a dealer extra he would be able to find you a car, but the fact was, for most people, you had to keep fixing your old car.

At various times during the war we had drives to help the war effort. As a Boy Scout, I participated in paper drives and scrap drives. (Now, when I think of the Model A, and Model T Fords that we picked up in groves and turned into scrap, I cringe, knowing what those cars and parts would be worth today.) As a Girl Scout, my sister, Judy, participated in drives to collect milk weed pods, to be used to make parachutes.

One of the favorite drives that I had a part in was the "Victory Garden" drive. I'm sure that this was a directive which had come down from Washington, and was designed to have people in the cities increase their production of food. The drive was connected with the school. We students, who volunteered, were to take pledge cards around the neighborhoods and have people promise to plant a garden, to alleviate the food shortage. As luck would have it, I was paired with Virginia Bishop, an upperclassman, and one of the prettiest and nicest girls in school.

It was not hard for me to be diligent in canvassing our assigned neighborhood. But the response we got was questionable. Most people scoffed at our cards, saying that they had always planted a garden, and they didn't see why this year would be any different. But most were gracious enough to sign our cards and we ended up with a respectable number of returned cards.

After Pearl Harbor and the initial setbacks during the early phases of the war it became increasingly apparent that we would win the war, and the speculation became, rather, just how long it would take. There was no television, so we could not watch the progesss live, but we did listen regularly to Edward R. Murrow on the radio, read the newspapers with great expectation, and watched the newsreels at the theater, which showed the war in moving pictures, and were updated each week.

In 1945 the <u>Omaha World Herald</u> carried a feature on its front page, which showed a map of Germany, and each day pictured just how far the Americans on the West, and the Russians, on the East, were from Berlin. While Patton was allowed to run free the Americans were advancing at twice the rate of the Russians. It was during this time that a fellow at the barbershop was heard to proclaim, "At the rate they're going now, I doubt that the war will even last for the duration!" But of course Patton was reined in, and the Russians were allowed to take Berlin and Eastern Europe, and 45 years of the Cold War followed. But that is another story.

Now that Memorial Day nears again, I'm looking forward to going back to Plainview once more. I'll take part in the services at the cemetery, with that beautiful display of American flags, and give my thanks, first hand, to our soldiers, living and dead, who responded to the call when they were needed. Then I'll wander through the cemetery, and mingle with the spirits of family and friends who rest there. And I'll remember about the days when we did our part in winning the war on the home front in Plainview.

THE PACE OF WAR

When the war began, it came with a suddenness that caught everyone by suprise. True, looking back at the events leading up to WWII, there were unmistakable signs that the disaster was imminent, but American and Japanese delegates were talking peace in Washington right up to the Sunday, December 7th, when the Japanese bombed Pearl Harbor. I'm sure that our people in Washington thought that the talks would go on and on. Certainly those of us at home thought that way.

Loring (later Scraper) Jenkins was one of the boys at the bakery in Plainview when the war began, and his situation was in many ways typical of the "Pace of War". Immediately, with many others of that age, Loring wanted to enlist, to serve his country. His choice was the Marines, but instead of being called up after his physical, he was told to go home and wait for instructions. He did and became terribly frustrated when he heard nothing for what he thought was a very long time. Then one day he got his orders to report the very next day for assignment. He was truly in a dither. He hadn't packed, and he had to say goodbye to his girl, and his mother etc etc etc. This was his first experience in the Army's (or Marines') first rule, "Hurry up, and Wait". Really, that was the "Pace of the War" for all of us. Always the same story, feverish activity, followed by long periods of waiting for something to happen.

(Note: Loring was a standout athlete at PHS and was a fellow I admired and looked up to. His exploits on the playing fields were legendary, and his natural friendliness, quick wit, and wealth of stories made him a favored companion. After school and Saturdays I looked forward to accompaning him on deliveries and assisting him in his duties at the bakery.

I've always thought that the ebb and flow of service life, the bursts of activity and the lulls, suited Loring very well, and his subsequent career as a professional baseball player bore that out. The excitement of the battle (not that he or anyone ever enjoyed battles) was akin to the excitement of the game, and the long periods between events were times of banter and comaraderie--in contrast to the steadiness of the usual 9-5 job where the only excitement comes with the weekly pay check. Even within the baseball game there were periods of no activity (on the bench between innings) followed by intense activity at the plate or a stolen base. Both the action and the inactivity (banter) he found enjoyable.

Loring, to my knowledge, was the only person ever to conduct a strike at the bakery. At the time, he was making $10 per week, and from that $10 Ella Myers, the bookkeeper, would withhold 10 cents for Social Security. When Ella would give him that handful of change he would argue that he should have the entire $10. One day he announced that the 10 cent deduction was unacceptable and if anyone was interested he would be at the Pool Hall, on strike. He didn't try to influence anyone else to join him, but he did want to make a statement. My Dad later caught up with him and persuaded him to come back to work. Whether he ever got his ten cent raise or not I'm not sure.) End of note.

One event stands out to illustrate the "Pace of the War" for me. It was a lazy summer day in Plainview and several of us were lounging on the bank corner, trying to decide what to do. Nothing much was happening anywhere in town. Then, literally out of the blue, came a B-17, flying so low that we thought the wings would scrape both the bank building and the Frost Block across the street. One thunderous moment, then it was gone, carrying our friend, Gene Hecht, to his fateful rendezvous with death in Europe.

For three and a half years the war ground on and on and on. Little hopes would be followed by long periods of disappointment. Rationing of food, gas, and tires conserved products, but made people edgy. More and more men left for the service. Usually, they left in groups. After a little send-off they would be gone, then for a long time, nothing. The little blue star flags in windows of homes signifying a serviceman began to multiply around town. After awhile people would complain about no mail from their service man, then a whole packet of letters would come at once. Or, "Please God No!" the dreaded telegram-- "We Regret to Inform You..." Some of the blue stars were replaced with gold stars.

In the spring of 1945 our one constant during the war, Franklin Delano Roosevelt, died at Warm Springs, GA. The nation mourned, and wondered if Harry Truman, whom nobody seemed to know much about, would be able to direct the war to a successful conclusion. More waiting. Then, suddenly, in June, the war in Europe was over. The celebrations were tempered by the realization that the war still waged in the Pacific.

During the summer of 1945 my Mother and sister and I were in Kansas City. The news of the war dominated the papers and the radio. Our boys were having success in the Pacific, but it seemed as if we were going to have to invade every little island, one at a time, and the fanaticism of the Japanese soldiers previewed a bloody battle when it came to the Japanese mainland. Washington authorities were warning that casualties on both sides would be worse than anything we had seen before. Each day the Kansas City Rail Station was gorged with troop trains carrying GIs across the country from assignments in Europe to ports of embarkation on the west coast for the coming invasion of Japan. Once again it looked as if the war would last for a very long time more.

Then, on August 6th, Col. Paul Tibbets and his crew took off from Tinian in the Enola Gay and dropped the bomb on Hiroshima that changed the world. Three days later another, more powerful bomb was dropped on Nagasaki. The war was over. Who knows how many thousands of lives, both American and Japanese were saved. We thanked God. Harry Truman had passed his test.

Kansas City went crazy. A half million people came out, and all of them seemed to congregate on 10th St. in front of the Muelebach Hotel. It was pandemonium. The streets were clogged with people. No automobile traffic was able to move, though those trapped in their cars honked their horns until their batteries were spent. Bottles of liquor were passed from hand to hand, never to return to the original owner. Girls, pretty or not, were kissed and kissed some more. Servicemen were hoisted on the shoulders of civilians and imprompto parades were formed. Guests in the upper floors of the hotels threw towels and toilet paper and buckets of water from the upper floors, and even those doused in the process merely laughed and waved. Shouts of "Its over!" and "Victory!" were nonending, and everyone waved the two finger victory salute as they moved slowly, more or less north to south along the street.

The celebration lasted most of the night, and though I'm sure there must have been fights and acts of vandalism there was very little of either and no complaints from the merchants or police afterward.

The biggest problem we had was the next day when we tried to get something to eat. Almost everyone took the day off, and the only restuarant downtown that was open was the Muelebach Coffee Shoppe. The line waiting to get into that place extended entirely around the block, and by the time we got in the only items on the menu were hamburgers, without buns, and coffee. We were grateful to get even that.

A few days later, General Eisenhower passed through Kansas City and gave a speech at the park near the rail station. At that moment General Ike, the hero of the European campaign, was probably the most popular man in the world. His greeting to us, which later became familiar during his political career (both hands raised high over his head, and that wonderful grin), was greeted with wild shouts and thunderous applause. In his speech he attempted to put the events of the last 3 and a half years, and especially the last 3 and a half months, into perspective for us. He warned us that the task of winning the peace would be every bit as hard as was the winning of the war. He was right of course, but at that moment we were all still basking in our moment of victory. The cold dawn of reality and decades of dealing with the Cold War would strike us later.

BUSINESSES IN PLAINVIEW

Note: Some time ago there was an item in the Flashbacks column of the News which mentioned that a new oven had been installed at the Plainview Sehnert Bakery, in the building which now houses Barbara Young's antique store. This was especially interesting to me because that same week, 50 years later, we were installing a new oven in our bakery in McCook. Since that time I have thought about that old oven a good bit, as follows:

THE OVEN

The heart of any bakery is the oven. When my father and mother bought the bakery in Plainview, from Sam Johnson, in 1930, there was a very small, inefficient oven in place. My Dad was young, ambitious, and determined to expand the business of the bakery. The existing oven was a real problem, and limited any expansion, so just as soon as he could afford it, he set out to buy a new oven.

Revolving ovens were new on the market in the early 30's, and there was much controversy over the baking qualities, the speed of baking, and the economics of the revolving oven as opposed to the old reliable hearth oven, which of course had been around in one form or another since man first began to bake bread. Its reliability and baking quality were unquestioned. Furthermore, the hearth type was the oven Dad had grown up with in Presho, SD, and had used in his first bakery at Ft. Pierre, SD. and he was very comfortable with it. It really was the very best when it came to baking bread, and bread was to be the principle product of the Plainview bakery. And the versatility of the revolving oven was not yet proved.

So after much agonizing, he decided to buy a streamlined version of the old hearth oven. It was a beauty, at least the part that showed in the bakeshop. It had a bright white enamel front, with shiny instruments for indicating the time and temperature, and had chrome handles and levers for adjusting the steam going into the oven, dampers for regulating the heat, and the like.

There were two doors opening into the baking chamber, but the baking chamber itself was just one large domed space, lined with white fire brick. Baked products were placed in the oven and distributed throughout the chamber by the use of an oven peel. This oven peel was a flat wooden retangle about 10 inches wide, 18 inches long, and 1/2 inch thick, which was fastened to a wooden pole about 8 feet in length. The front edge of the peel was sharpened so that the baker could slide the peel under pans of bread or rolls and move the pans around the oven chamber, or bring them to the oven door.

From the door of the oven the pans of bread (4 bread pans were strapped together as a unit) were grabbed by the baker, using oven mitts on his hands, and the bread was dumped onto a dump rack. From here the individual loaves were placed onto a wire bread rack to cool. The usual method of loading an oven of bread was to have one baker handle the peel and to have a helper place the pans on the oven ledge for the peel handler to manuever into the oven. Unloading reversed the procedure. This required considerable team work, but two skillful bakers could load and unload a rack of bread in a suprisingly short time. My Dad and Bill Riddle, an excellent baker who had served his apprenticeship in the army during WWI, could do a commendable job of handling both the pans and the peel alone, but a novice

175

would always find himself tangling with the long wooden peel handle or knocking someone or something about with it.

The real difference between the Ft. Pierre oven and the new one in Plainview, besides the chrome and the greater capacity, was the way that each was fired. In Ft. Pierre my Dad used bundles of willows, burned directly in the oven chamber to heat the oven. These willows would be allowed to burn down to ashes. Then the ashes would be raked out of the oven into trash cans. The oven would be swabbed clean with a damp gunny sack, and the ashes carried to the alley--a very hot, slow, disagreeable process.

In Plainview, the oven was fired with coke, into a furnace chamber at the back of the oven, from a room separate from the bake shop. Across the alley, south of the bakery was the coke pile where my Dad stored the coke that fueled the oven. During these years my Dad bought his coke by the traincar-load. When the carload arrived it was delivered from the railcar to the bakery by draywagon. The load made a great mound in the back of the bakery. We boys had great sport climbing this jagged mountain, and we imagined high adventure as we trudged up our black Mt. Everest, and enjoyed a picnic lunch on its summit. I can still feel how very uncomfortable it was sitting on those sharp coke cinders, but it must have held great attraction for us, perhaps because it was so very uncomfortable.

Note: (Coke is a fuel made by burning soft coal in a limited air supply. The resultant product is very porous and brittle, and contains a high concentration of carbon. It is hard to light, but once ignited it burns very hot with almost no smoke.)

176

The fire in the oven burned continuosly. After the baking for the day was completed the fire had to be banked in a certain manner so that it burned slowly, but did not not go out. My mother used to make good use of the fact that the oven was always hot, if not up to actual baking temperature, and frequently baked roasts, or batches of lentils or stew in the oven during the day for our evening meal.

There were clinkers (spent coke) formed during the burning process that had to be removed during the banking procedure, and these were transported to the alley in a wheelborrow, dumped on the road surface (over the years the alley built up a fine hard surface, not unlike the cinder running tracks popular at schools of that era). A fresh supply of coke was brought into the furnace area on the return trip of the wheelborrow. This was very hard, hot work, and the furnace stoker worked up a great sweat. Johnny Logan, and later Merton Grecow performed this job after they returned from their bread route to Brunswick and towns to the west.

In Fort Pierre, before moving to Plainview, my Dad did come down with pneumonia and almost lost his life. My folks always attributed this to his task of taking the ashes out in the dead of winter. We must have had hardy souls in Nebraska, because, though they grumbled considerably, to my knowledge, no one became ill going in and out of the furnace room in Plainview.

There is a gas, however, that is given off by the burning coke that is very disagreeable, and under certain weather conditions there would be a particular down draft, and my Dad would be laid low with a sick headache. These headaches were enough to send him to bed, and had it not been for his strong constitution and great determination, I am sure they would have driven him out of the bakery business. I don't remember his ever missing a day's work, though I remember many a Sunday when he would be too sick to leave his bed. But come early Monday morning, he woud have made a miraculous recovery and be right back on the job.

When the bakery moved across the street in 1944, to the corner building now occupied by the Plainview Automotive store, there was no consideration given to installing another hearth oven, and there was a collective sigh of relief throughout the bakery when Dad announced that the new oven was to be an oil fired, automatically controlled revolving oven.

BUSINESS NEIGHBORS

By the time I was aware, in the 30's, the cheese factory, the soft drink bottling plant, the cigar factory, and the taxidermist had come and were gone, but Plainview still had a core of essential businesses and prided itself on being rather independent. As one of the merchants remarked one day, perhaps a little too smugly, "If you can't find it in Plainview, you don't need it!" Maybe it was because we didn't realize all was available in the world, but we generally believed that statement.

We had two meat markets in town, Kuhl's (formerly Saathoff's), and Fisher's. Both of these markets did their own meat processing, and each featured sausages with special seasonings, in which they took great pride, and each commanded a loyal following. As a child I knew these merchants well, and visited their stores regularly. If I accompanied my mother on a shopping trip they would often reward me with a wiener out of the case, to be eaten on the spot, but if I was alone they would visit and be friendly, but would rarely offer a sample of their wares.

P.F. Boyens had a very large and well stocked furniture store on the north side of Locust St. Mr. Boyens had come to Iowa from Germany as a young man in 1880. By 1887 he had arrived in Plainview to work in a general store. In 1894 he opened his own furniture store, and a few years later added the undertaking business. He was a very progressive business man. In 1913 he purchased the first motorized hearse in the state of Nebraska. This was a vehicle he designed himself, and was manufactured by a company in St. Louis. The body was made of oak, and weighed some 4,800 pounds. It

179

created a great stir in the undertaking business and letters of inquiry were received from all over the midwest.

My friends and I loved to browse through the furniture store, and if we could get away from the watchful eye of Nemo Ashburn, would bounce on the sofas in the basement. But better yet, we liked to visit the embalming center in the building in back of the store (now the Senior Center). Russell and Rex Boyens, grandsons of P.F., were my age, and would give us a guided tour. Rex had a vivid imagination and enjoyed making us squirm as he described the burial preparations and pointed out the instruments that were used.

In a tiny building, just west of the furniture store Deck Grafe had his tailor's shop. Deck was one of Plainview's earlier settlers, coming to the community from Germany in 1889. Deck never married, and never learned the English language very well, but if you caught him in the right mood he would visit at length, in his thick German accent, not stopping his sewing, but looking up and laughing occasionally as he recalled something about "Der Alt Country. He was a good tailor and retained a loyal following of older men, who had their suits hand made, even through WWII.

Deck lived at the Johnson Hotel and took his breakfast at Maurice White's Corner Cafe (across the street from Steinkraus Oil Station.) Deck was the first person I ever knew who wore a toupee. It was not a very good toupee. It was brown, with an artificial reddish cast, and didn't fit very well, at best. But in the morning when he came in for breakfast the toupee would frequently be decidedly askew, sometimes with the part extending from one ear across his head to the other ear. No one, that I knew of, ever ridiculed Deck to his face, but at these times there was always a good bit of merriment over trivial matters, as patrons attempted to conceal the real object of their mirth.

Bob and Harry Johnson operated a harness shop on Locust Street, across the street from the Johnson Hotel. The feature of that store that fascinated me and every other child was the life size model of a dapple grey Percheron horse. This horse was outfitted with every piece of harness that the Johnson boys made, bridles, blinds, collars, fly netting, the works. Other harness pieces hung on hooks on the walls. Buggy whips stuck up straight in a barrell on the floor. Their leather working machines were lined up along one side of the store. All of the harness was well oiled, and the smell of the oil and leather was unique and very pleasing.

Bob and Harry were probably past middle age when I knew them. They were avid sportsmen, and hunting and fishing were very important in their lives. By the middle thirties their business was primarily the repair of shoes and some fixing of harness because there was very little new harness being sold. I loved to poke around in that store and watch as they worked with the leather, on one or another of the many machines in the shop.

When one took a pair of shoes into the shop for repair, the brothers would be quite short, and not very friendly. I got the idea that they didn't care for people very much. They did good work, but didn't have time for small talk. That was for certain.

Then one time I had a harness problem. At a farm sale, my Dad had gotten a harness for our shetland pony, Nicky, for use on a cart and sleigh. The problem was that the harness was too large for the small pony, and I was asking Bob Johnson if there was anything that he could do about it. You would have thought that I had brought him a Christmas present. For the first time I saw him open up. He assured me that there was no problem in adapting the harness, and showed me how certain parts had not been taken care of properly and should be replaced, and then instructed me on the proper way to oil and maintain the harness. He was a totally different man than the cranky fellow who looked after my shoes. As he took measurements of the pony he laughed. He joked. He reminisced about the old days when the demands for their harness were so great that they had to hire extra help.

After they remade that harness Bob and I became quite good friends, and even Harry was passably friendly. They never failed to ask about the pony and how the harness was fitting, and if I was taking care of it like they'd instructed me. It was sad. Here were two craftsmen, who had been successful in their business, and had loved their work. But they were in a situation they could not control. Times had changed. They knew it. People had stopped using horses for farm work. There was no demand for their harness anymore. They were too old to change. They had shifted to the repair of shoes out of necessity, but that was not the work they loved, and they never did fully adapt to the modern world.

OUR DAILY BREAD

When my folks bought the bakery in Plainview, in 1930, the large wholesale bakeries had not yet begun to saturate the market with daily deliveries of bread and baked products to every hamlet in the country. Indeed, in country towns like Plainview, people depended primarily on the local bakery to supply the bakery products that they did not make at home.

But times had already begun to change, and the Sehnert Bakery began to take advantage of that change. For instance, some of the small towns around Plainview had already lost their local bakeries and my folks began to wholesale baked goods (mostly bread) to some of the grocery stores and restaurants in surrounding towns. For the towns immediately to the west, Copenhagen, Brunswick, Royal, Orchard, and Ewing, they established a route, and for a number of years serviced those towns with their own vehicle. Initially this vehicle was a Chevy van. Later a small truck was used, on which was mounted a custom-made large, heavy square box in which shelves were arranged from floor to ceiling to hold boxes of bread or pans of rolls and donuts.

Johnny Logan, who was working at the bakery for Sam Johnson when the bakery changed hands, was the first deliveryman I remember, and for a number of years handled the "west" route. Before I started to school and summers I used to accompany Johnny on the "route". This was a special treat as Johnny was a favorite of mine, and everyone else for that matter. He was good natured, and had a ready smile and good word for everyone he met. He joked a lot with me and let me "help" with the deliveries, though of course at that age my help consisted mainly of opening doors and running back to the truck for things he'd forgotten. But he made me feel important, and I felt privileged when I got to go along.

At that time Johnny was not yet married, and seemed to be on very good terms with all of the young girls who worked in the stores where we stopped. I'm sure that we lingered longer at some of the stops than my Dad would have thought necessary, but when Johnny was around there was always a lot of laughing and people always felt better for his being there.

I especially liked the drive out of Brunswick, going on country roads to Ewing. Just south and west of town the trees on either side of the road were huge and their branches met to form a great green canopy high above the road. It was like driving through a tunnel, and no matter how hot the day was, it was always cool and quiet along that stretch of the trip.

Later, back at the bakery, Johnny had his chores to perform, and I liked helping with that too. He always removed the clinkers from the old coke oven, banked the fire, and brought a fresh supply of coke into the furnace area. He also carried 100# sacks of flour up 6 or 7 steps onto a platform above the bread mixer so that flour could be sifted into the mixer in preparation for the next day's run. He was not a very big fellow, but he must have been strong, as that was very hard work.

And of course there were always pots and pans to clean, and usually a few in-town deliveries or errands to run. But Johnny never complained and always seemed to be in a good mood. We looked forward to a daily radio program in which Garry Moore and Durward Kirby sang, and bantered back and forth, engaging in lighthearted highjinks in the skits they presented. We laughed together and Johnny would sometimes make a note of one of the jokes so that he might share it with one of his friends on the route next day.

In addition to the route that we ran to the nearby towns to the west we also sent bread to the towns further west via the railroad, Verdigre, Niobrara, Verdel, Lynch, Bristow and Spencer. For these orders we would pack bread in cardboard boxes, tie the boxes up with twine, write the addresses on the boxes with a crayon, then take them to the depot where they would be loaded aboard the morning train. For a number of years my folks did business with stores in these towns, and had never met most of the customers. Usually there was a standing order that was sent out on a regular basis. If the order was to be changed, or there was a special order, the people would convey that information on a postcard. Phone calls were rare, if at all.

Once, on one of our annual trips to South Dakota to visit relatives, my Mom and Dad made a special effort to stop in all of those towns to meet their customers in person. It was an unusual trip as these people, here-to-fore only referred to as "Niederost Store", or the equivalent in the other towns, suddenly had faces and immediately they became friends, sharing the common bond of commerce; they, too, had wondered about people who made the bread from Plainview.

One thing that was unusual in all this packing of bread for shipment by rail was that the bakery never did buy packing boxes. I'm not sure that my Dad would have known where to go had he wished to buy any. Instead, he was entirely dependent upon other merchants to keep him supplied with boxes. One of my chores at an early

185

age was to pick up boxes after school. The grocery stores provided us with some, as did the furniture store and hardware store. But the most dependable source for boxes for the bakery was the J.C. Penney store. Every day, it seemed, they had a supply of nice, clean boxes in which they had received merchandise. We were careful to pick these up on a regular basis before they were taken to the alley to be burned. Occasionally would we find a sweater, or shirt in a box that had been overlooked in unpacking, which we would dutifully return.

Dean Allen, the manager of the Penney store was a good friend of my Dad, as were Dale Crawford and Van Weston, who came later, and they were very good to instruct their clerks to call us before throwing out good boxes. The process over the years must have saved the bakery thousands of dollars; it probably made that entire shipping operation feasible.

As a boy, the concept of the Penney store led to some confusion on my part, of which Berniece Allen, Dean's wife, reminded me years later. In the small town I was personally acquainted with most of the store owners. Mr. Goos and Mr. Houston ran the grocery stores that bore their names. Mr. Ebinger ran Ebinger's Hardware Store, and Mr. Baber ran Baber's Cafe, and of course Mr. Sehnert had Sehnert's Bakery. So when we were visiting in the Allen home one evening I managed to confront Berniece alone in the kitchen. "Mrs. Allen", I asked, "Do you think it's right for you to live in this house with Mr. Penney?"

Eventually the railroad ceased to have a dependable enough schedule to make shipments of bread practical so that part of the wholesale business was curtailed. The war pretty much stopped the route to the west. When Wausa, Osmond, and Randolph lost their bakeries it was decided to concentrate on those towns, and the route to these towns was continued until my folks retired in 1965.

As with most things in a small town, the delivery route had its personal aspect as well. On Highway 20, between Plainview and Osmond lived an elderly couple, the Rice's. At that time they did not drive very much, so Mrs. Rice arranged with my Dad that if she hung a dishcloth on a pole outside her kitchen, then he was to stop on the way back to Plainview, as this would be the signal that she needed something from the bakery (and a little conversation and news from the outside world). The system worked well, and helped the Rice's to stay longer on the farm.

But after the war everything was in a state of change. Instead of making individual stops for bread, meat, and non- prescription drug items, the grocery stores became a one stop haven for the busy housewife. And people, long deprived by the war of choices, now took advantage of the choices that were available, and this included choices of bread and rolls, and even the town where people would shop.

My Dad enjoyed his role as the supplier of baked goods for the community, and worked at that role seriously. He took it personally when he saw a friend or customer with a loaf of shipped in bread, and would be very upset with the people at the bakery, suggesting that they were not making the product good enough, or were not friendly enough to the customers.

After one Chamber of Commerce meeting, at which ideas were discussed about ways that the merchants could keep the customers at home instead of making the 30 mile trip to Norfolk, Dad and one of the workmen, who had just completed a sizeable job at the bakery, were hashing over the situation. Dad asked the fellow why he didn't buy the Plainview bread; didn't he like it? "Oh, no, Walter, it's not that at all. It's strictly economics. With those three boys of mine, when I put out a loaf of your bread they will finish the entire loaf at one meal. With the shipped in bread I only have to buy two loaves a week!" And this was at a time when bread cost 10 or 15 cents a loaf.

Part II
OUR DAILY BREAD

Selling bread wholesale was by no means the most important part of the bakery business in Plainview in the 30's. From the beginning the retail portion of the operation was the key to the bakery's success. Men who worked downtown regularly stopped for a loaf of bread, or rolls, or cookies on the way home for lunch, or the evening meal. And Saturdays were extremely busy as this was the one day of the week that farm families made their trip to town.

From the very beginning, in 1930, my folks were blessed with good employees (for the most part), hard working, honest, and loyal people who worked to make a good product, and keep the bakery clean. Bill Riddle, a World War I veteran, was an excellent craftsman who worked well with my Dad in the early days. Bill was a bachelor and took his noonday meal with our family. He delighted us with his stories about the army in France, and sometimes brought his souvenirs for us to examine.

He had one habit which I never could understand. No matter what we had for dessert, Bill would regularly finish his meal with one or two slices of bread liberally covered with gravy. If it happened to be a meal at which there was no gravy he poured cream and sugar over the slices of bread. Somehow, that, with a cup of coffee, was necessary to finish a meal.

We always had young women who worked in the front of the bakery. In addition to waiting on the customers, their duties were many and varied. They frosted the rolls, iced the cakes, and put up orders. They also were responsible for wrapping the bread. Until the mid 30's the bread was not sliced. Since this was long before the era of plastic bags, the material of choice for wrapping bread was waxed paper. The loaf was placed into an adjustable form which assisted the operator to make the proper folds in the paper, then the loaf was slid into a heated chute which melted the ends and the bottom of the paper, then on into a cooling area where the wax on the paper would set up and seal into a package which could be handled. The wax paper was good to keep the the bread from drying out, and the wrappers were wonderful to make the slides in the park slick and fast.

In about 1935 my Dad bought his first bread slicer, a reciprocating blade slicer which worked very well, except that the machine almost had to be torn down to replace the dull blades. This operation required a great deal of patience, skill, and care to keep from being cut by the slicer blades.

Most of the young women who worked at the bakery came from farm families, but some were "queens". It must have been Roosevelt's Inaugural in 1937. We were listening to the account of the Inaugural Parade on the radio. One of the clerks had participated in a beauty contest at the County Fair the previous summer. As the announcer described the thousands of people lining Pennsylvania Avenue and cheering the President's motorcade she lounged over the counter, and had a faraway look in her eyes as she said, "I know just how he feels. That's the way it was in Neligh last summer when they crowned me Queen of Antelope County!"

There were many of these farm girls who worked at the bakery over the years. I'll tell about just one. Ella Meyers came to work for my folks while we still lived above the bakery. She was shy and at first her duties were to look after my sister and me, and clean the apartment while my mother worked a shift at the bakery. Gradually she began to assume bakery duties, and eventually replaced my mother at the bakery, so that Mom could spend more time at home.

Ella was a very thorough worker. She kept things clean, and she kept orders straight. She also had the patience to operate some of the more stubborn machines. The automatic donut machine soon became her special project. She could keep it in adjustment, protected the cutter from becoming dull, and kept the machine scrupulously clean. When the bakery got an automatic bread wrapping machine, Ella was the one that kept that in top working order as well. When she would go on vacation there would always be trouble with those two machines getting out of adjustment.

Ella was quiet, always did her share of the work, and worked well with the other people at the bakery; and, as is the case with willing workers, over the years she assumed more and more responsibility in the business, and was almost a part of our family. She stayed at the bakery until the time my folks retired. Some years after my mother passed away Ella and my father were married, and for more than 20 years we've been proud to have her as an official member of our family.

In 1944 my folks bought the Houston Grocery building (now the Auto Supply) across the street from the bakery on Locust Street, and proceeded to move the bakery. It was a very good move, to a double building, so not only was there more room, but my folks had the luxury of laying out the bakery so that there was a smooth flow of production. With a new rotary oven, new freezer, and new pan washer, the work was definitely easier and more pleasant.

Before the bakery was moved, and while the building was completely empty, Dad hired a one-man band and invited everyone to a dance at the new bakery. Dances were always popular, the "band" was good, and the idea of a dance at the bakery must have had some appeal, so there was a good crowd and we all had a lot of fun before the carpenters started remodeling the building into the new bakery.

In a small town, we did not have a lot of tourist business, and when a stranger did happen in clerks would take the time to find out who they were and ask about their trip. My mother would tell them about Chilver's Park, and even buttered the bread for their sandwiches. Some of these people would send Christmas cards, and remember, with thanks, the friendliness of the people in Plainview, Nebraska.

But mostly, the bakery, and every other business in town, was dependent upon repeat business from a small base of customers. To keep these customers happy we all took pains to treat them well. If a customer wanted an order delivered to her home we accomodated her. Many customers took advantage of this service, and, I'm afraid, many times also took advantage of my Dad. Sometimes a lady would call up for only a half dozen rolls, or one loaf of bread and want it delivered. If this order came after the regular deliveries were gone the girls might ask Dad if they should call back and say that this delivery was not possible. Invariably, Dad would answer that he would drop the delivery off on his way home.

There was also the matter of paying for these orders. If a customer did not happen to have the right change, the order would be charged, and sometimes these charges would add up to a sizeable amount over a few months. Collecting these overdue charges was distasteful work, and my Dad was very poor about making collections. He listened to the hard luck stories, sympathized, and came away with no money. Then it would be left for my Mother to collect. Once or twice a year she would gather up a stack of overdue bills and set out to collect. She was very good at this job. She had a knack for not letting the issue become personal. She assumed that, of course, the person wanted to pay, and indeed had just been waiting for her to present the bill. She not only would come home with the money for the overdue bill, but frequently she would have been invited in for coffee and a little friendly chat.

And so it was, in that other time. The pace of business was slower. Nobody was getting rich, but our relationships with the people we worked with, and with our customers, was more personal. And those friendships, which developed because of commerce, remain as treasures of the past.

HOTELS

Plainview has always provided good accommodations for travelers. Before the term "motel" was even coined we had accommodations for folks traveling Highway 20. In those days we called them Cabin Camps. But long before that Plainview had hotels that catered to the traveling public who early on came mostly by rail.

There were three hotels with which I was familiar during my time in Plainview, from 1930 to 1957. The first, The Commercial House, later renamed The Grand, the oldest of the three, was a white frame, two story structure, nearly as old as Plainview itself. When it was a hotel it was located one block north of the depot, at the location now occupied by the Carhart Lumber Co. Years ago, before World War I, plans were made to demolish the building to make room for the Lumber Yard.

Instead of tearing the building down, as the contract read, the contractor decided to cut the building in half, from roof to foundation, and make each half into a single family dwelling. One half was moved east two blocks, and the other east five blocks. I know that the venture worked out well, because my wife and I lived comfortably in one of the houses for four years and were very happy. Lee Jordan's parents lived in the other house, which was later destroyed by fire.

One day while we were living in our hotel-house, an old gentleman knocked on our door and said that he would like to walk through our house, as he had stayed there many times when it was a hotel. As we visited in our living room, which he said had been one half of the lobby-dining room, he fascinated us with stories about the old days.

He had regularly traveled through Plainview, on the train, one of many traveling salesmen, or drummers, as he called them. He remembered that one table always had a white table cloth, and was adorned with a large bowl of fruit. Diners sitting at this table were charged 50 cents for their meal, while diners sitting at the plain tables were charged 25 cents for the same meal.

After the evening meal the drummers would sit around in the lobby and swap stories about customers in towns up and down the rail line, exchange tips about the best places to stay and eat, and tell anecdotes about the people they had met. The sessions would last into the wee hours.

On one visit to the Commercial House, the old timer told us, he had a very important appointment up the line at Spencer the next day, so it was necessary for him to catch the early train. The night clerk, a rather empty headed chap, assured him that he would give him a wake up call. Sure enough, the next morning there was an urgent pounding on his door.

"Are you the fellow that has to catch the 6:57?", the clerk asked, a bit sleepily.

"I sure am", was the reply.

"Well, it's a quarter after 7 now and the train's gone," the hotel man said.

"Then why are you telling me now?"

"Well", drawled the clerk, "You sounded like it was important and I thought you'd want to know."

The second hotel was the Elks' Hotel, a modest lodging with some apartments, located on the second floor of one of the creamery's buildings, a block and a half north of the depot. This hotel was run by a Mrs. Roberts. Her son, Bob, was a tall, good looking boy, gifted with a deep rich voice. While in high school, he had a magic act, with Marvin Tepner, that was great fun and very popular. The two boys were in great demand in and around Plainview, to provide entertainment at various events, and Bob frequently doubled as the Master of Ceremonies.

Later Bob moved to California, and as Bob Warren, achieved a certain fame as an announcer and actor on radio and early television programs. His big break came when he was chosen as the national spokesman for a new car that the Ford Motor Co. was introducing--the Edsel. Fortunately, for Bob, he was also the announcer for the Lawrence Welk show. I still take satisfaction, every Saturday night, in seeing Bob, there on the screen, having a high old time, dancing with the ladies in the audience. Poor Bob, he'll no doubt spend eternity, announcing, smiling and dancing with the ladies, as the Welk show goes on an on, in reruns, year after year, forever.

The Johnson Hotel, the newest and largest of the hotels, was and is yet a two story structure that anchors the east end of Plainview's main business street (Locust). In the days before World War I, Andy Hansen and his partner, Frederick Austerlitz, operated the hotel and saloon, located in the west half of the building. In the summer Mr. Austerlitz's grandchildren would journey from their home in Omaha for a visit in Plainview. They were a familiar sight as they played on the second story balcony and on the sidewalk in front of the hotel and saloon. These two later danced their way to fame and fortune as Fred and Adele Astaire.

In the 30's Bill Johnson was the owner of the hotel. He was a tall, distinguished looking, man who operated a clothing store in the west half of the hotel's street level, where the saloon had been. He had an apartment in the basement of the hotel, but the management of the hotel was left to Mr. and Mrs. Green, who had their apartment on the second floor of the building.

Mr. Green was blind, and it was remarkable how he could register guests, visit with them, and put them at their ease. He operated his part of the hotel in a very civilized manner. He liked to go to bed early, so he left any of the guests who were still in the lobby in charge of registering late arrivals. When the last one left the lobby the keys to the vacant rooms were left on the counter with a sign that invited a prospective guest to help himself to an empty room and register and pay for the room the next morning.

Mrs. Green took care of the overseeing of the operation of the hotel, which included the maids and cleaning ladies, and the overseeing of the dining room (including a good part of the cooking, I'm sure).

The dining room was no doubt open for three meals a day, but the only meal that I knew about first hand was Sunday Dinner. There were some eight large round tables in the dining room, each of which would seat eight people. On Sunday these tables would be draped with gleaming white table cloths, and set with heavy restaurant silver. A highly starched napkin was folded in such a way that it stood up straight by the water glass.

The hotel dining room was popular throughout the area, and after church people would begin to arrive, to take places at any of the tables where there was room.

People were congenial. I'm sure that part of the charm of the place was that one never knew just who his dinner companions might be, so the conversation was always varied.

Everyone ordered his entree off the menu. There was always ham, and fried chicken, but after that there were three or four other main dishes that changed from week to week. There were individual salads, but the rest of the food, vegetables, relish plate, and rolls were served family style. The food was invariably good. It was appetizing, hot, and always carried the little extra touches that were Mrs. Green's trademark. {I was especially fond of her homemade jams and jelly, and the peppermint stick ice cream.}

Sometimes one of the specialties would be oversized frankfurters and sour kraut, served with a type of mustard that caused one's forehead to break out in a sweat. This was my favorite dish, and while it was hard for me to pass up the fried chicken and ham, I usually did, because I was afraid that the franks and kraut might not be on the menu the next time. It was not until years later that I learned that I was almost the only one that ordered the franks, and they usually put them on the menu just to please me.

After dinner, conversations begun in the dining room would be continued in the lobby of the hotel, which at that time was furnished with a couple of sofas and a number of large wooden rocking chairs.

Ordinarily, I was very impatient when my parents would linger to talk, but not at the hotel. Mugs (Margaret) and Betty McHenry were nieces of the Greens and were always at the hotel for Sunday dinner. These two girls were a little older, and much wiser than I. They

197

were very bright, and had vivid imaginations, and when they were around there was much laughter. At their home, on the south edge of town, they had ponies, and a barn with a hayloft, trees to climb, and a feed mill across the street. It was an ideal place to play, but the hotel was not bad either.

The girls kept a supply of board games and books upstairs in Aunt Mable Green's apartment. Sometimes they would read to my sister and me, or we would put on a little play. Other times we had races down the long halls of the hotel. Mugs was a real tomboy, and had the knack of getting you to think you could do things that were really beyond you. One time she called attention to the fact that the steel poles that held up the second story porch were just like the poles that city firemen slid down when responding to a fire call. Before I knew it, I had volunteered to be the first to slide down one of the poles, in my Sunday duds of course. Unfortunately, I chose the pole that was right in front of the window where my mother was sitting. She was very surprised to see me slide past. That was one time when the conversation in the lobby came to an abrupt halt.

The Plainview Creamery

The Plainview Farmers Cooperative Creamery came into being in 1926, formed by a group of local farmers who were interested in improving the profitability of their dairy operations. George Lingenfelter was the first chairman of that committee and Chet Christiansen, a local real estate and insurance man, was appointed the first business manager.

The immediate aim of the group was to begin the manufacture and marketing of butter made from their raw milk. J.C. Wade was hired as the first butter maker, and named manager of the creamery in 1929.

Under Jay Wade the local creamery developed into a sizeable operation. It purchased cream and eggs from a wide area. It had local delivery of milk, and first and foremost, it manufactured Pride O' Plains butter. In the manufacture and the marketing of this butter, Jay Wade proved to be an innovative manager and a salesman of great merit. He quickly realized that the Plainview facility had the ability to produce much more butter than the local populace could consume, so he began searching for markets beyond the immediate geographic boundaries.

As the 30's progressed the Plainview Creamery began selling butter in large quantities on the eastern seaboard of the United States. Jay had an ingratiating personality, and when he noticed that a number of the butter brokers were Jewish he immediately took steps to assure those brokers that the Plainview product was indeed made in a manner which would qualify it as being Kosher.

One of the byproducts of the butter was the buttermilk. During these years the creamery sold this buttermilk as a semicondensced product, as well as in the dry form. Both products were used for hog feed, and both involved driers. When the dryers were working, and the wind was from the south, the smell was terrific, and was not at all pleasant. (On one occasion, at least, students at the high school petitioned the principal to dismiss school, saying the smell was too bad to hold classes, to no avail). As one of the local merchants said, "That is the smell of industry, and business for Plainview!" As far as I know, there were few formal complaints, in those pre-EPA days.

One year, during the 30's or 40's, I remember that 1 million pounds of butter were shipped out of Plainview for the east coast. But that large volume of butter soon depleted the volume of cream for butter that the local farmers could supply. This led to a larger and larger territory that the creamery trucks covered in their quest for raw material for the Pride O' Plains Butter. One of the innovations that Jay brought into being to help both the local economy and to alleviate the creamery's shortage of milk was the annual "Calf Sale". For this sale truckloads of fine quality milk calves were shipped in from Wisconsin and sold, at cost, to local producers either to form the basis of a new herd, or to strengthen the quality and numbers of an existing herd. A number of young farmers were helped in getting their start in the dairy business through this program.

The annual meeting of the Creamery Co-op was one of the big events of the year. In the early years the Creamery Board would have a gigantic free pancake feed, which would be followed by a Co-op members' meeting at which a progress report would be given and the dividend checks handed out. All of the local merchants would have Pride O' Plains specials on that day, and a festive atmosphere would prevail.

The board did not seem to restrict the attendance at the pancake feed to Co-op members only, and a great many of the students would hurry their lunch hour to have a round of pancakes and sausage before school started at 1 o'clock. One year Ray Pendergast and I got so caught up in entering the line for a second and third time that we decided just to skip the afternoon at school and went to the annual Co-op neeting instead. As I remember that meeting there was a good bit of applause as the progress report was given, but then it developed into a rather numbing recitation of incomprehensible figures of which we quickly tired, and since we had already pigged out on the pancakes we were at a loss as to what to do for the rest of the afternoon.

Sometime after the end of the war, Jay Wade's flamboyant personality, which was largely responsible the the great success of the creamery operation clashed with the conservative nature of the majority of the board members, and Wade's long association with the Plainview Creamery came to an end.

In the early 30's Plainview had a number of small dairy men who delivered milk and cream from door to door. This of course was unpasteurized, unhomogenized milk which came in a glass bottle. After a short time the cream came to the top of the bottle and this was skimmed off to be used in coffee and on cereal. The milk that could not be sold at retail was separated, the cream to be sold to the creamery or one of several produce men in town, the skim milk to be fed to livestock. Skim milk, as

I remember, was not considered suitable for human consumption.

Later in the 30's, as health requirements became more strict, the creamery gradually supplanted the small dairies and took over the home delivery business. These home delivery men sometimes got involved in situations totally unconnected to the milk business. (No, I'm not going to tell any milkman jokes.) I remember that one time Earl Butterfield (isn't that an apt name for a dairyman!) was busy on his route when he came upon a young man rolling over and over on the grass, in obvious pain. A young woman and her mother were near hysterics, trying to help him. It seems that the boy and girl had had a lovers' quarrel, and to spite her, he had taken poison outside her door. With great presense of mind Earl forced volumes of cream from his truck into the boy's stomach, causing him to throw up the poison and at the same time coating his stomach to the extent that he saved the boy's life, to love again, with happier results, at a later date.

Following the departure of Jay Wade, the creamery management went through several changes, with varying results. In the middle 50's Gib Millnitz was named manager, a position he held until long after we left Plainview (in '57). Gib had worked at the creamery from the time he got out of high school in the early 30's, until he left for the army in 1944. When he returned from service he went to work in Bob Bush's automobile agency until 1954, when he returned to the creamery as general manager.

It was during Gib's tenure that the creamery probably reached its greatest growth. In addition to the Pride O'Plains Butter and the retail milk business, the creamery bought additional driers and entered the manufacture of non fat dry milk as well as buttermilk solids, began marketing eggs and animal feed, and even began the processing and freezing of poultry. At the peak of their operations some 60 people were employed by the Plainview Cooperative Creamery, making it by far the largest employer in town. For many years it stood as a most positive economic force for the community. Many individuals, even families, spent their entire working lives at the creamery.

BAKERS' NARCOLEPSY

Narcolepsy is a not so funny disease that nevertheless has sometimes comic symptoms. It is characterized, outwardly at least, by the victim's falling instantly asleep, at any time, any place. When we first moved to McCook one of the banks had an officer who was afflicted with the disease. He was finally forced to retire. It is very disconcerting to be earnestly laying out your need for a loan and suddenly your banker starts snoring across the desk from you.

Another friend of mine has narcolepsy. He seem perfectly normal, but if someone tells a funny story and he begins to laugh heartily, sometimes he will fall instantly asleep, and if standing at the time, will collapse to the floor. He can not take a bus (alone) for transportation lest he sleep through his stop, and a five minute cab ride in a strange city might find him asleep four of those minutes.

These are unfortunate cases of real narcolepsy, which if not constantly treated with medicine, can have disastrous consequences. The similar affliction I want to talk about is Bakers' Narcolepsy. This has to do with people who work at night, especially for long, long hours, and get their circadian clock out of whack. The circadion clock is our biological 24 hour cycle that tells us to sleep at night and stay awake in the daytime. Most people experience this dysfunction as jet lag after long flights over many time zones.

Bakers, who work nights, experience it frequently, and especially on Saturday nights and Sundays after a grueling night and day of work. It seems especially to be triggered by the sound of organ music and the voice of a minister as he begins his serman, as anyone who has had the misfortune to sit behind a baker in church can attest.

However, a baker does not have to be in church to suffer the effects of Bakers' Narcolepsy. The Sehnert women have learned that it is wise and safer to take the wheel initially on a trip in the car. Until becoming accustomed to days and nights as normal people, driving is torture for a baker. Coffee is the medicine of choice, and bakers seem to have a great affinity for that beverage, the stronger the better.

My father, a lifelong baker, has always had a great talent for dozing. He has had trouble staying awake at concerts amd lectures. amd regularly slept through the movies on Saturday night. He has been known to fall asleep while visiting with insurance salesmen, or even invited guests in his own home. One time he and I attended the State Fair in Lincoln, and after tramping through every livestock barn, we decided to check out the "girlie show" on the midway. Even I was shocked when I looked over to see how he was reacting to the girls' strip tease. I found him, head bowed, snoring softly, fast asleep.

A faulty circadian clock can sometimes lead to bizarre circumstances. One time my Uncle Rudy, a baker at Holdrege, and my father made a trek to South Dakota to visit relatives. They were both exhausted by the time they got to Yankton, so they decided to stay overnight and resume the trip the next morning. They chose to stay in a rooming house, and retired about ten in the evening. Since neither carried a timepiece, the owner offered to lend them an alarm clock. Rudy said that that would not be necessary as he would wake up at the proper time (6 a.m.) on his own. That would give them just the right amount of time to get the Huron, 125 miles away, in time for breakfast. Sure enough, Rudy woke up at his usual time, then shook Walter, my Dad, awake. The two were completely refreshed from their sleep, and prepared to leave. The owner met them on the stairs. It turned out that it was still only 2 a.m., and he thought they were absconding with his valuables in the middle of the night. Of course they arrived in Huron long before normal people were getting up, so they were forced to doze (and grumble as to whose fault it was) in the car outside the relatives' home until they could properly present themselves for breakfast.

The Nebraska Bakers always had their annual Association convention on a weekend in October... a Saturday evening dinner and dance, and all day Sunday meetings and demonstrations. It was common to see one or two bakers at each table dozing for a few minutes, or longer, at the dance on Saturday night. At the meeting on Sunday afternoon a speaker needed to have whistles and a brass band to hold his audience's attention.

One time it was decided to change the format of the convention slightly. After dinner on Saturday night an instructional film was shown. Five minutes into the film there was not a baker left awake, and only the wives were left to learn "A New Technique For Changing Bread Slicer Blades" from the film. It was generally agreed, however, that the dance that year was the most successful in years, as all the bakers seemed to have gotten a fresh surge of energy from their 30 minute nap.

My Dad and I, both bakers, have been known to fall asleep in the dentist's chair, even without hypnosis, and more than once we have dozed off and dropped our

206

fork, halfway to our mouth, at a family dinner. We regularly fall asleep in the barber's chair, and it was here that I found out that our strange malady is not restricted to bakers. One time, in Plainview, I was getting my hair cut and of course immediately took my little nap. When I woke up and looked into the mirror, there was Ozzie, my barber, posed with scissors and comb over me, like a vulture ready to strike, fast asleep on his feet. I cleared my throat. We both chuckled self consciously and he resumed my haircut.

Sometimes this Bakers' Narcolepsy can be dangerous. Once one of my Dad's new bakers was frying doughnuts. As he was waiting for the doughnuts to be ready to turn, he fell asleep and allowed his hand to drop into the hot grease. He awoke instantly, but not before he suffered a nasty burn. Needless to say, he never fell asleep frying doughnuts again.

I'm not sure, but this ability to fall asleep instantly may be hereditary. My son, Matt, now the active baker in the family, has the ability, and his daughter, Gretchen, one and a half years old, also has the knack. I'm fearful. I think I see a familiar pattern developing. Hopefully, it is something she will outgrow...if we can keep her out of the bakery.

SPECIAL BOOK SECTION

105 YEARS (PLUS 2)
OF CORNHUSKER FOOTBALL

Rarely in the 100 plus years of Cornhusker football have Nebraskans looked forward to the season with more optimism than we do in 1994. The near miss for the gold ring of a National Championship on January 1, 1994 in the game against Florida State in the Orange Bowl is viewed by many in the state as a building block on the stairway to a #1 ranking in '94.

So this seems like a good time to review the progress of the Cornhusker team, its history, and its legend, over the past 105 years, to see just how we happened to get to this point in time.

Without further adieu, let's talk a little football.

Nebraska football can be divided into 3 distinct eras; 1. The early years, culminating with the Rose Bowl game on January 1, 1941.

2. The Dark Ages, beginning with World War II and ending in 1962 A.D.(After Devaney)

3. And the Golden Age of Nebraska Football, the years, beginning in 1962 A.D. to the present.

The Early Years

The first game of football involving a team from the University of Nebraska was played on Thanksgiving Day, 1890, against the Omaha YMCA. Yes, even in those days there was critcism about the patsy schedule that the team maintained. But we won that first game, 10-0, and things were off to a good start. The first Nebraska coach was Dr. Langdon Framingham, who had come to Lincoln from one of the Ivy League schools, and brought a football with him. The first captain of that first team was Ebenezer Mockett. These two names sound a bit formal, in light of some of the later coaches, with names like Bummy Booth, Jumbo Stiehm. Indian Schulte, and Potsy Clark.

The 1890's and early days of the new century naturally saw a good many firsts.

* The first paid coach was Frank Crawford who received $300, in 1893.
* The first black player was George Flippin, 1891-'94. Flippin was a very good player and led Nebraska to a 6-0 victory over Illinois in '92. His presence on the team caused Missouri to forfeit a game in Lincoln in 1892.
* The beginnings of long lasting rivalries were established. Most of the teams that now make up the Big 8 were played in those early years.
* Nebraska also played the Indian schools. A scoring record of 119-0 was established against The Haskall Indians in 1910, but The Carslile Indians, with the great Jim Thorpe, trounced the locals 37-6 in 1908.
* Nicknames, Bugeaters, Black Knights, etc. were tried then discarded. Finally, in 1902 Cy Sherman, of the Lincoln Star referred to the   team as "The Cornhuskers", and that name stuck.

The new century brought Coach Bummy Booth to Nebraska. He was a product of the east, from Princeton, and he knew his football. He also had great talent, the likes of Maurice Benedict, John Westover, and most of all, Johnny Bender, '00,'01,'02,'03,'04. Bender was a very fast and elusive back, and set the standard to which all the speedsters at Nebraska since that time are still compared. Under Coach Booth, Bender starred on undefeated teams in 1902 and 1903. The 1902 team achieved a record of 9 wins-0 losses. What is more, no points were scored upon them the entire season, the only time in Cornhusker football history that this has ever been accomplished.

Even though Booth's teams won almost all of their games, they did lose to Michigan and Minnesota, so Booth was forced out. "He couldn't win the big one!"

One young Nebraska coed, Willa Cather, was a great football fan, and regularly covered the team in stories for the school paper. She later described football on the University of Nebraska campus of that day in her novel, "One of Ours".

The teens brought Jumbo Stiehm and his Stiehmrollers, headed by football star, Guy Chamberlin. Stiehm, who was called Jumbo, not because of a huge stature, but rather because of his unusually large feet, liked his players small and fast. He was hailed as an organizational genius, a strict disciplinarian, and a great recruiter. With greats like Clint Rose and Vic Halligan anchoring the line, and speedy, tricky backs like Len Purdy, Max Towle, and Dick Rutherford he proceeded to build a powerhouse at Nebraska. In addition, there was Guy Chamberlin, who could do it all on the football field. He was a punishing runner, and a fearless blocker. But he also passed, caught passes, punted, drop kicked field goals, and was a devastating tackler. Knute Rockne commented, after the Irish had gone down to defeat in 1915, "Without Chamberlin, Nebraska would be easy. Chamberlin is a team in himself!"

Later in the 1915 season, after Chamberlin had scored on a 38 yard pass, a 3 yard plunge, and a twisting 51 yard dash, in a 33-0 pounding of Kansas to clinch another Missouri Valley title, one writer exclaimed, "In the good old days, Jessee James and Quantrill were considered bad men around Lawrence, but if you ask somebody on these streets this evening, they will tell you that Guy Chamberlin is the worst bandit who ever galloped through this town!"

In 1916 Coach Stiehm left for Indiana when the University of Nebraska refused his request for a salary of $4250. The student newspaper, The Cornhusker, said in eulogy: "For Stiehm, it was not enough that Nebraska have a good team; he early established the ideal for which Nebraskans would strive--**Never to Suffer Defeat**. He jerked the blindfold of timidity from Cornhusker eyes. With Nebraska awake to her full strength and potentialities, and aided by the constant influx of new material, he gave Nebraska three years of unbeaten football."

The twenties were the decade of the Athlete-Hero. Across the breadth of the land people idolized Babe Ruth, Jack Dempsey, Red Grange. Here in Nebraska, we had our heroes as well; Clarence Swanson, Link Lyman, Clare Sloan, Blue Howell, and most of all--Ed Weir.

During a ten year period, Nebraska teams under Coach Fred Dawson, then E.E. Bearg, defeated Illinois and their great star, Red Grange. They defeated Notre Dame, with George Gipp. They also beat Notre Dame two out of three times while the Four Horsemen were writing their own bit of football history. There were wins over Pittsburg and a number of eastern schools. As the Cornhuskers gained prominence nationally, their popularity grew in Nebraska to the extent that they outgrew their old stadium. The new stadium, "Memorial Stadium", was completed in 1923. Fittingly, Nebraska

212

defeated Oklahoma, 24-0, in the first game played in Memorial Stadium on October 13, 1923.

One player who played a huge part in this success was Ed Weir, from Superior. He was listed as a tackle, but he had a way of always showing up where he was needed. He carried the ball on offense; he blocked; he punted; he threw passes; and above all, he was a rock on defense. After the Notre Dame game in South Bend in 1924, Coach Knute Rockne demanded to be let into the Nebraska locker room. He walked over to Ed Weir, who was in a near state of exhaustion, grabbed his hand and said, "Young man, that was the greatest exhibition of football I've ever seen!" And this was after the one defeat that Weir's Cornhuskers suffered at the hands of the Irish.

The 30's were good years for Nebraska football. University officials had tried to lure Knute Rockne away from Notre Dame when E.E. Bearg left, but Rockne declined, recommending Coach D.X. Bible of Texas A.& M. Bible was credited with selling the team to the state. One of his first acts as head coach was to tour the state from one end to the other, explain what he was trying to do, and ask for support. The result was that the Nebraska people no longer recognized the Cornhuskers as the University's team, but looked upon them as "Our Team".

Bible's early teams were dominated by two fine backs, Bernie Masterson and George Sauer, both of whom later coached in the Big Eight. These two played together at Lincoln High, and were able to brag that they never lost a game in their hometown all the while they were in high school. What is more, they played together for three years at the University of Nebraska and were able to claim that they never lost a game in Lincoln during that period either.

Sauer was a strong runner, and Masterson was a fine blocker and passer. He was also something of a character. They tell this story of Bernie Masterson, when he was playing quarterback, in the pros, for the Chicago Bears:

George Halas, the legendary coach of the Bears, thought that Masterson was being a bit too cute in his play calling in a game that was pretty much wrapped up. "Now I want you to go in there, run three off tackle plays, and then punt. We'll hold them on defense", Halas instructed.

So Masterson proceeded to follow those instructions to the letter. The first play gained some 30 yards right down the middle. The second play gained another 15 yards. The third gained 25, and carried all the way to the 2 yard line. Without a moment's hesitation, Masterson lined up in punt formation, and proceeded to punt the ball clear out of the stadium. Of course Halas yanked Masterson out of the game, and was almost beside himself with rage as he asked, "What were you thinking out there?" Masterson was said to have replied, "Well, Coach, I was thinking, that's the craziest series of plays that **you** ever called!"

The teams of the mid 30's, still under D.X. Bible, dominated the Big 6 Conference and ranked in the top 5 of the nation. Two standouts of this period were "Wild Hoss" Lloyd Cardwell, and Sam Francis, Mr. Outside and Mr. Inside. Cardwell didn't care much for practice, but how he could run. Fred Ware, of the Omaha World Herald, gave him his nickname. He wrote of Cardwell, "It's his roaring, tearing, gay freebooting way that reminds

214

me of the defiant, joyous, speeding wild horse of the prairie that loves to run with the wind." Everyone knew that when "Hoss" got the ball he was going to run a sweep, but it didn't matter, because following a Sam Francis block, he usually outran the defenses anyway. He was also a something of a free spirit, and caused the coaches considerable grief because he had the habit of stiff arming a tackler, WITH THE BALL!

Bible left for Texas in 1937 and was replaced by Colonel "Biff" Jones. Jone's teams continued the dominance of the Bible teams, and his career reached its zenith in the Rose Bowl game on January 1, 1941. The Rose Bowl game perhaps is over emphasized in Nebraska history, but it certainly has served as the focal point of Nebraska football for the last 50 years. One fellow, who moved here from out of state, said that he lived in Nebraska for 3 years before he found out that Nebraska actually lost the Rose Bowl game.

That year the whole state was caught up in the Rose Bowl fever. The team made the trip to California by train, stopping at Phoenix to practice for a few days. Another special train carried many of the 5,000 fans to California for the game, for $58.95, round trip. Almost at the last minute, it was decided to take the Nebraska band. The Chancellor would approve the band trip only if it could be an educational experience, so for 10 days the band journeyed to California, via the train, with side trips to Mexico and San Francisco, in addition to marching in the Rose Bowl parade, and taking part in the half-time festivities.

The Rose Bowl game marked a number of changes, not only for Nebraska football, but for all of college football. It matched a good big Nebraska team with a superb line, anchored by All Americans, Warren Alfson and Forrest Behm, against a smaller team with finesse, Stanford. Stanford's coach, Clark Shaughnessy, had installed the T formation, and in Frankie Albert, he had the quarterback to make it work. It was a great game. Veteran sportscasters, Graham McNamee and Bill Stern both referred to it as the greatest game they had ever seen. But in the end, deception and speed overcame strength and brawn, and Stanford won 21-13.

Another aspect of college football died with the Rose Bowl game. This was the last Nebraska team to be made up entirely of Nebraska boys. Notre Dame, Army, Navy, and the various pre-flight programs at a number of universities, during the war, proved the value of nationwide recruiting. It also marked the end of innocence in College Football in America. The players on that team, as well as those all across the land were mostly in the military before another year passed, and many would never come home. After the war college football became big business, and probably never again will be quite so much fun.

The Dark Ages

But after the Rose Bowl came World War II, and with it came the Dark Ages for Nebraska Football, which lasted until 1962. Colonel Biff Jones, and most of the Nebraska players were called to service. There was a veritable drought of talent on the campus of the University of Nebraska. Ad Lewandowski, a former Cornhusker football great, was working in the Nebraska Athletic ticket office. But he was needed, so he agreed to serve as Head Football Coach, and Head Basketball Coach, as well as Athletic Director.

On the field Lewandowski was short as well. During the war, one squad was made up entirely of 4-F's and 17 year olds. These players were long on heart, but short on talent. A long bleak era for Nebraska football had begun.*

    * Footnote to Nebraska Football History: In 1945, one of those 17 year olds was a 141 pound end that you won't read about in any other history of Big Red football. His name was Walt Sehnert. And just a word in defense of "Patsy Schedules". In 1945, NU played South Dakota toward the end of the season. The game was pretty well in hand before the end of the 1st half. That was the signal to start using the reserves. So for over half the game, the scrubs mopped up the remains of the South Dakota team. In those days the crowds were not as large as they are today, but they cheered with as much enthusiasm, and to the end of my life, I'll remember that glorious afternoon when I lived the dream of every Nebraska kid, when I played in Memorial Stadium for the Nebraska Cornhuskers! Already that fall, veterans had begun to return, and by spring practice it was apparent that if I were to continue to go to the games free, I would have to join the band. So for the next 3 years, I rooted for the team from behind my baritone in the Cornhusker Band. *(end of footnote)

    There was a succession of coaches during this period, none of which was outstanding. George "Potsy" Clark was head coach on two different occasions. His contribution to Cornhusker lore consisted of quips--he was the most entertaining coach speaker up to the time of Bob Devaney. He also inserted one notable play into the playbook, called the "Platte River Spread", a mile wide and one inch deep.

217

Most of the highlights of this era are really lowlights, for instance:

1. The shoddy way that Biff Jones was treated after the war.
2. The player rebellion under Coach Bill Glassford.
3. The 0-6 loss to Hawaii in 1955. This was a team that Nebraska had trounced 50-0 the year before.

But there were 3 bright spots for the Cornhuskers from 1941 to 1962, namely:

1. Tom Novak
2. Bobby Reynolds
3. The Big Upset of 1959

Tom Novak played at the end of World War II. Off the field he was a real nice fellow, but he played football like a man possessed. His nickname of "Train Wreck" was earned. Like Guy Chamberlin, he earned All America honors at both center and fullback, but it was as a defensive specialist that he was at his greatest. He made his tackles straight up, chest to chest, eyeball to eyeball. Against Notre Dame, in 1948, he made over half of the team tackles, and at the end of the season, the Notre Dame squad voted him "The Best Player they had played against that entire season".

Because of injuries his last two years that restricted his playing time, Bobby Reynolds really had but one season, 1950. But what a season it was. As a 19 year old sophomore, Reynolds rewrote the Nebraska record book, scoring some 22 touchdowns, and gaining over 1300 yards, both phenomenal achievements at that time, and for the first time in many years, Nebraska climbed into the top ten football ratings.

Reynold's trademark was his knack for reversing his field, and his run against Missouri still ranks as one of the greatest runs in Nebraska football history. The play started from the Missouri 33, and eventually Reynolds scored, but not before he had retreated to his own 40 and reversed his field at least 3 times. They tell this story about Charlie Toogood during that run:

Toogood had thrown a block on a Missouri man, and then lay on the fellow. The Missouri man protested, "Let me up, the play's over".

"Not necessarily", Toogood replied. "Bobby might come back this way again!"

The third bright spot of this era was the Big Upset of 1959. The team at this time was coached by Bill Jennings. Jennings was a good recruiter, and the players he recruited formed the nucleus for Devaney's first teams. He had a good personality and the players liked him. It was in coaching where he had his troubles. In 5 years he won a total of 15 games. It is ironic that two of these victories were over perennial champion, Oklahoma.

In those days, the Big Eight was referred to as "Oklahoma and the 7 Dwarfs". The Sooners, under Bud Wilkinson, had not lost a conference game in 13 years, and Nebraska had not beaten them in 17 years. The Sooners had not lost in 75 conference games! Nebraska, on the other hand, entered the 1959 game with a 1-5 record.

And yet, it was one of those days. Nebraska was led by little Pat Fischer, of the famous football Fischers, out of St. Edward, Nebraska. Jennings had also inserted an ingenious formation for that game, "The Double Quarterback", where two men would line up under the center and dash off in different directions. This day, that was enough. The Cornhuskers pulled off the "Impossible Dream" and defeated the mighty Sooners 25-21.

When the crowd at Memorial Stadium got over the shock, they went wild and ripped the steel goal posts out of their concrete bases and paraded them down "O" street in downtown Lincoln. Later the goal posts turned up at the ATO Fraternity House on campus where the boys cut them up into 1/2 inch chunks and sold them to the public as souvenir paperweights.

Then, just to prove that the '59 victory was no fluke, Jenning's 1960 team, this time with police protection, beat Oklahoma again, 17-14, in Norman. But these "Once in a Blue Moon" victories were not enough, and after the 1961 season, Jennings was through at Nebraska. He went on to Coach at Kansas and Wasburn, saying that expectations for a nationally ranked football team at Nebraska were too high. With our small population base and limited budget, we should be satisfied to compete in the Big Eight and not worry about the national picture. The eastern press agreed with him.

Then along came Bob!

The Golden Age

Bob Devaney came to Nebraska from Michigan, by way of Wyoming. Immediately things began to change. First, he toured the state, speaking to groups, as thoroughly as D. X. Bible had some 30 years before. With his infectious good humor and Irish wit, he proceeded to bring the state together. Before Devaney arrived, there was a real grassroots movement in the panhandle to secede from Nebraska and become part of Wyoming. People felt as if they had nothing in common

220

with the rest of the Nebraska. As soon as the Cornhuskers started winning that talk became less and less until today it is rarely heard at all.

One indication that Devaney was successful in his efforts in barnstorming the state is indicated by this story: When Bob Devaney first came to Nebraska there was considerable debate over whether the name, Devaney, should be pronounced "De vain'ey", or if it should be "De van'ny". The mystery cleared up fast when someone came up with the slogan that soon swept the state, "Get up off your fanny, and Help Bob Devaney!".

Bob Devaney says that to be a successful, a coach must make it seem as if he is leading a parade, even as he is being run out of town. After the team began to win, Devaney says that people began to refer to him a "Sweet Old Bob". After he suffered through two 6-4 seasons, in '67 and '68, those same people began to use just the initials, and "Sweet Old Bob" became "S-O-B".

Now, we Nebraskans take for granted the things that for decades were just statistics for other programs at other Universities to achieve; things like winning seasons, annual bowl games, All American candidates, Heisman and Lombardy Trophy winners, and full crowds at Memorial Stadium. But before Bob Devaney came to Nebraska, these things were rare indeed.

The high point of Devaney's career occurred with the back to back national championship teams in 1970 and 1971. The 1970 team entered the Orange Bowl ranked 5th in the AP poll. All of the teams that were ranked ahead of the Huskers that day lost their bowl games, and Nebraska vaulted into the national championship on the strength of their 17-12 victory over #3 LSU.

The 1971 season featured the "Game of the Century", the win over Oklahoma. Nebraska and Oklahoma had been ranked #1 and #2 all season, and the suspense had been building. Nebraska had a very steady team, led by Jerry Tagge, Johnny Rodgers, McCook's Jeff Kinney, Rich Glover, and Lombardy Trophy winner, Larry Jacobson. Oklahoma was led by Jack Mildren and Greg Pruitt. But the real star for Oklahoma was the "Wishbone Formation", and in those early days of that formation, no one was really certain that it could be successfully defensed.

This was truly a battle of two great teams. There were great plays on both sides. Most memorable, perhaps, from a Nebraska standpoint, was Johnny Rodgers' darting, twisting return of a punt for a touchdown, early in the game. And who could ever forget the picture of Jeff Kinney on that final drive of the game. He had already scored 3 touchdowns, and on this drive, his jersey was all but torn away, as he carried the ball four straight times from inside the 10 yard line, to go in for the winning touchdown. That jersey, or what is left of it, is proudly enshrined in the McCook High School trophy case.

After NU had defeated Alabama and Bear Bryant in the Orange Bowl, 38-6, the final AP ratings for the season showed:

#1 Nebraska #2 Oklahoma #3 Colorado
Truly, this was a singular achievement for the
Big Eight Conference.

Bob Devaney is considered one of the great coaches of all time. He is in the Hall of Fame, and rightly so. He had the ability to surround himself with great football coaches, men like Tom Osborne, and then

222

he had the good sense to let them do their thing. His personality allowed him to have his way with University authorities, the boosters, and of course, made him one of the all time great recruiters.

Tony Jeter tells this story of the time that Devaney came to recruit him: Devaney, Tony, and Tony's Dad were in the kitchen talking football. Tony's mother was in the living room, playing hymns on the piano. Devaney excused himself, went into the living room, motioned for Mrs. Jeter to keep playing, and was soon singing the hymns while she played. After that, Tony said, his mother would not hear of his going any place but Nebraska.

Devaney's personality has made him a very successful politician here in Nebraska. That trait has served him well as a coach, where he handled a good many temperamental players. One of these was Bob Brown, later an All American at Nebraska, All Pro lineman with the Oakland Raiders, and a 1994 enshrinee in the College Football Hall of Fame. Brown once thought that he might quit the team, as football was just too rough a sport. Devaney agreed with him, and suggested that Brown might switch to tennis, and together they discussed the possibilities of Brown's earning a living on the tennis court. Brown soon changed his mind, and concentrated on his football career.

Devaney was able to walk a very fine line in the matter of Johnny Rodgers' troubles with the law. He was able to negotiate with the authorities, to satisfy the law, and yet not ruin the career of a gifted, but headstrong young man. He succeeded, and Rodgers went on to become NU's first Heisman trophy winner.

Even more, though, Devaney's personality and ability to focus on an objective, has made him a most successful athletic director.

As Nebraska's AD, he spearheaded two expansions of Memorial Stadium, complete with a state of the art Press Box.

The Bob Devaney Sports Center was built, a model facility of its kind which serves the people of Nebraska for sports and entertainment the year around.

He has engineered a women's sports program for the University which is renowned throughout the country. All of the sports at Nebraska have been upgraded so that now the Cornhuskers are competitive in all areas, while complying with the NCAA rules and regulations.

Above all, he has lent his weight to the football program, and kept the Stadium seats full.

When Wyoming opens the '94 season at Memorial Stadium the game will mark the 195th sellout for a home game, an ongoing NCAA record. Fans are loyal, and take their presence at the games seriously. The story goes that Bob Devaney was walking around inside the stadium one game day, when he looked up and saw an empty seat. He went into the stands and found an elderly woman in the adjoining seat. When he asked her about the empty seat she explained that it belonged to her husband, and that they had held these seats for years, and now her husband had died, so she had to come alone. "I'm sorry, maam", Devaney said. "But couldn't you have given his ticket to one of his friends?" "Oh, no", she replied, "They're all pall bearers at his funeral today".

Each football Saturday people start converging on Memorial Stadium from all over the state. They start the trip at midnight in Scottsbluff. They're picking up donuts in McCook at 5 a.m. when the bakery opens. From north and south they converge on Interstate 80, till that arterial becomes a river of Red clad fans flowing toward Lincoln. At service stations, all along the way a prediction of the score is displayed in large letters, rarely, if never predicting a Cornhusker loss. Later in the day the cars take to the road from the east, and at last all converge upon Lincoln from every direction, disgorging passengers, who by game time will make Memorial Stadium the third largest population center in the state of Nebraska, behind Omaha and Lincoln, but ahead of Third City, Grand Island.

Season tickets to the games are jealously guarded. In divorce cases they have been a major point of contention. Ticketholders who have left the state religiously pay for their tickets, only to turn them over to friends living in Nebraska. Provisions in wills provide for the payment of tickets long after the ticketholder is gone, because a University policy prevents transfer of tickets to another party. Any unpaid for tickets must be returned to the general pool of tickets.

In many instances fans have held the same tickets for so many years that the people in a particular section become close friends, traveling back and forth to graduations and weddings, and family occasions. These friendships are good, held together by the common glue of the love of Cornhusker football.

In 1973 Devaney turned over the head coaching duties to Tom Osborne. During these past 21 years Osborne has become the winningest coach in the land. He has gained a national reputation as a great football mind, and as the director of a clean and successful football program. He has stressed academics among the players, and Nebraska has placed more Academic All Americans than any other school. His teams have never won fewer than 9 games a season.

Still, Osborne suffers criticism because his teams are too slow; they don't pass on first down; they are too predictable. Yet this is the same fellow who came up with the "Bummerooski" and the "Fumblerooski", surely two of the most unusual of trick plays. But he has never won a National Championship, and he hasn't won a bowl game since January 1, 1987. "He just can't win the big one!", his critics complain.

Osborne has suffered the criticism with stoicism as he continues to correct his team's weaknesses, recruiting for speed, training the players for strength and agility, and fine tuning his basic offensive and defensive schemes. For the most part he keeps silent instead of answering his critics directly. There are times, however, that his rebuttal is barely contained beneath the surface and ready to explode.

In 1986, prior to a game with Illinois in Champaign, an old friend of Tom's brought his father to meet the coach. In the conversation it was brought out that the father had owned tickets to the games in Lincoln since the 30's, had not missed a home game in years, and that this day was his 95th birthday. "Well", said Tom. "You really are a fan. I think we should do something special for you today. What would you like? Should we pass on first down? Second down? Heck, maybe you'd like us to pass every down."

"No, Mr. Osborne", said the old man with some feeling. "That won't be necessary. I think you're doing just fine!"

Probably Osborne's most outstanding team was the 1983 team, which featured the triplets, Turner Gill, Irving Fryer, and Mike Rozier, who produced "The Scoring Explosion", and came within a hairbreadth of winning a National Championship. In the Orange Bowl on January 1, 1984, against the University of Miami, Nebraska scored at the end of the game to make the score Miami 31-Nebraska 30. An extra point would probably have sealed the National Championship for the Huskers, since they would have had just the tie to blemish their record, against one loss and a tie for Miami. However, to Osborne's credit, he never hesitated, but immediately called for a two point conversion. The pass, from Turner Gill to Jeff Smith was barely tipped and the National Championship slipped away to Miami.

There was a good deal of conversation over Osborne's decision to go for the two point conversion, and gloom throughout the state was akin to that suffered by earthquake or tornado victims, and hotlines to psychologists were installed for counselling. However, most people agreed that Osborne was right in his decision to go for the win. Later that year, Osborne went into the hospital for a single heart artery bypass, which turned out to be a double. At a celebrity roast soon after, one of the jokes was: "Isn't that just like Tom. He had to go for two--again!"

Dr. Tom's degree is in Educational Psychology, and he uses that degree to the utmost. He has developed a walk-on program that is the envy of every coach in the country. Somehow, he gets his players to make the most of their talents, and maybe a little more. We've been blessed, here at Nebraska, over the years by having players who played above their ability:

227

* Eddie Schwartzkoph played guard on the Rose Bowl team, at 160 pounds.
*Frank Solich was a 158 pound fullback who set a single game rushing record of over 240 yards.
* Jeff Kinney, the hero of the game of the century, was supposed to be too slow to play for a Division 1A school.
* Kenny Walker achieved All America status and earned a Pro contract with the Dever Broncos, even though he is deaf.

These players and so many more are over achievers who have left their mark on Cornhusker football, and in the process have made loyal fans out of almost all of us throughout the state.

In 1993, with Bob Devaney's retirement, Bill Byrne took over the office of the Athletic Director at the University, and assumed responsibility for taking Nebraska Athletics into the 21st Century. Formidable problems loom on the horizon:

1. Budgetary problems abound as the athletic dollars have to be divided to cover more and more men's and women's sports.
2. Compliance with NCAA requirements.
   a. Restrictions on the number of scholarships that can be given for football and basketball.
   b. Restrictions on the number of assistant coaches
   c. Curtailment of recruiting visits by coaches
   d. Balancing the number of women's and men's sports.

Coupled with these vexing problems, which promise to be with us for years ahead, was the immediate problem of "Nebraska Bashing" by what seemed to be a conspiracy of the nation's newspapers and sports commentators.

The problem, according to many writers and sportscasters, stemmed from a number of factors:

1. Though Tom Osborne had become the winningest coach in the nation, he had lost 6 straight bowl games.
2. He had never won a national championship.
3. The Nebraska regular season schedule was looked upon as weak.
4. The brand of football played at Nebraska was dull- not enough passing.
5. The team was seen as big and strong, but the players were slow.
6. The weather, late in the season was too cold and blustery to pass the ball, so we were forced to rely on the run in order to compete in the Big 8. That made defeat in the Orange Bowl inevitable, since there we would be facing one of the super fast, passing teams from Florida.
7. Conclusion: Nebraska should forget about getting a National Championship for Coach Osborne.

Shades of 1962 all over again!

As the '93 season progressed, the "Nebraska Bashing" approached the ridiculous. The Nebraska team had adopted the slogan, "We Refuse to Lose", and little by little the Huskers kept inching up the ratings ladder, till toward the end of the season, with losses by Florida State and Notre Dame on successive weeks, the Cornhuskers found themselves at the top of the coalition poll going into the Orange Bowl game against Florida

State. For some reason, this situation was unacceptable for many of the AP voters. Their vitriol was unvarnished. Nebraska had no business on the same field with Florida State, who was led by Heisman Trophy winner, Charlie Ward. The writers agreed that Seminole Coach, Bobby Bowden, was eminently deserving of the National Championship with his team, which many were referring to as perhaps the "Greatest College Team in History".

Thus, entering the Orange Bowl game on January 1, 1994, the Cornhuskers found themselves picked to lose by some 17 points, the largest spread of a game between the #1 and #2 teams in history. Somehow, somebody had forgotten to convince the Nebraska team that they were prohibitive underdogs. And they still had their motto, "We Refuse to Lose!"

After 60 minutes of football that night, many at the Orange Bowl and throughout the land felt that the Nebraska team had not yet lost. They had bested the "Greatest Team in College Football History" every place but in the record book, where the score is listed, Seminoles 18-Huskers 16.

Coach Osborne had devised a masterful game plan, and had prepared his team both physically and mentally. Charlie Ward, who had been sacked only 10 times in 11 previous games, was sacked 5 times, 3 by Butkus Award Winner, Trev Alberts. On numerous other occasions he was forced to hurry his throws, and at the conclusion of the game, of the two quarterbacks, it was Nebraska's Tommie Frazier who had played like a Heisman Trophy winner.

In the end, however, mistakes and penalties proved too much and the Huskers lost yet another bowl game and a chance at a National Championship when Bryon Bennett's kick sailed wide left as the final gun sounded.

The Nebraska players seemed to have known that the respect they sought could only be earned on the field. In that regard, their heroic efforts in the game against Florida State had been successful. The nation's sports' media were unanimous in their praise for the Cornhuskers in a losing effort. For the time being, "Nebraska Bashing " has been put on hold.

It remains to be seen if the resurgence of confidence will carry over to the 1994 season, and if the players will have retained their motto, "We Refuse to Lose". But as the Big Red Locomotive picks up speed into the Second Century of Nebraska Football, we are assured that the Cornhusker Spirit is indeed alive and well. Maybe '94 will be our year. We hope it is. Whatever happens, its great to be along for the ride.

Addendum: After the 1995 season

As expected, Nebraska opened the 1994 season ranked #1 by the Asssociated Press. Hopes were high for a good season, with a solid offensive line, proven defense, and a proven I back in sophomore sensation Lawrence Phillips. Above all, the team had the proven leadership of Heisman frontrunner, Tommie Frazier, at quarterback. The "We Refuse to Lose" boys, who had come up short in the 18-16 loss to Florida State in the Jan. 1, 1994 Orange Bowl game had a new motto, "Unfinished Business". For the first four games it appeared that finishing the business would be no problem, as they rolled past West Virginia, Texas Tech, UCLA, and Pacific by impressive margins. However, in the Pacific game came the first of what seemed to be disasters for the team. Tommie Frazier left the game with a calf bruise which turned out to be a blood clot behind his knee, and was thought to be a season ending injury.

Frazier's backup, Brook Berringer, proved to be an able replacement, until he suffered a collapsed lung in the 42-32 win against Wyoming. For the games against Oklahoma State and Kansas State, Berringer's playing status was severely restricted, and with third string quarterback, Matt Turman (the Turmanator), at the helm, the offense was largely limited to running Lawrence Phillips up the middle, and relying upon the defense to keep the opponent from scoring. But this was enough to dispose of Oklahoma State, Kansas State, and Missouri, though the physical misfortunes were enough to drop Nebraska to #2 in the polls.

Entering the game with Colorado the Cornhuskers were decided underdogs, but ended up completely dominating #2&#3 ranked Buffaloes, and won the game 24-7, and in so doing recaptured their #1 ranking in the polls.

The remainder of the season went along pretty much as expected, with a healthy Brook Berringer at quarterback. The offense sputtered at times, especially in the OU game, a 13-3 victory, but the defense picked up the pace at those times, and Nebraska ended the regular season with a record of 12-0, winning a fourth straight Big 8 championship. Tommie Frazier, injured since September 24th, suited up for this game, but did not play.

Going into the FedEx Orange Bowl against #3 Miami, a bit of the old "Husker Bashing" began to appear. Even though Nebraska was ranked #1, sports writers began to look at the Cornhuskers' record in previous bowl games, the lack of success against Florida teams, Miami's #1 defense, and the fact that Miami had lost only once in the Orange Bowl in the last 60 games. Many decided that Miami would win this one too. But Nebraska had a quiet confidence and some "Unfinished Business" to take care of.

Coach Osborne also had changed the picture somewhat. For the first time, on both sides of the ball, Nebraska had the players with the speed to keep up with the speedsters from Florida. He had also changed the practice schedule. Instead of taking off for an extended rest after the regular season, the Huskers began preparations for the Bowl game almost immediately, preserving their peak conditioning and timing. The thinking was that if the game was close in the fourth quarter Nebraska would be the stronger, more skillful team.

Miami was led by senior quarterback, Frank Costa, and the fine Miami defense was anchored by Lombardi Trophy winner, tackle Warren Sapp. The Miami players were confident that they would be able to run the Husker defense into the ground.

Until almost game time Osborne gave no hint as to who would be his starting quarterback. Brook Berringer had led the Husker charge through the heart of the season. Tommie Frazier, who had started out the season as a leading Heisman Trophy contender, was once more healthy. It was not until after the final scrimmage before the Orange Bowl game that Osborne announced that Frazier had graded slightly better and that he would start the game, but that both quarterbacks would play.

Through three quarters of the game it appeared that Miami would once more prevail. Nebraska played very well, but two costly interceptions, one by Frazier,

233

one by Berringer, kept Miami in the lead, 17-9, at the start of the final stanza.

But Nebraska's superior conditioning, and liberal substituting throughout the game were beginning to pay dividends. In the final quarter the Nebraska defense began to dominate the game. They had allowed Miami 143 yards in the first quarter, but only 132 for the last three quarters. Led by senior Terry Connealy, the defense swarmed quarterback, Costa, and the Miami passing game was ineffective for most of the second half. Offensively, Nebraska's line began opening up gaping holes for Frazier, Phillips, and Schlessinger to run. Schlessinger's two fourth quarter touchdown runs up the middle proved to be the margin of victory.

The players were unanimous in their praise for Coach Osborne. They lauded his ability to keep the team focused in the midst of adversity and seemed genuinely pleased at his finally capturing the elusive National Championship. And so it was throughout the state. Fans were ecstatic, and relieved that Coach Osborne could finally claim the one prize that had eluded him.

In the aftermath of the Orange Bowl victory Coach Osborne told of visiting Colorado several years previously to interview for the head coaching job of the Buffs. He had almost decided to take the proffered job, citing the discontent of the Nebraska fans. After all, he had never won fewer than 9 games, but it didn't seem to be enough, they wanted more and more. They were never satisfied. Then, while flying back to Lincoln, he began to think about those fans. They were never satisfied. But after all, he thought, he wasn't satisfied either. He didn't want to coach at a place where the fans were apathetic and ho hum about a less than perfect season. So he stayed at

Nebraska and vowed to to do his best to improve the Nebraska team. And in Miami, his efforts came to fruition. After 22 years of trying, and after 3 losses in National Championship games in Florida, Coach Osborne at last had captured that long sought prize.

The 1995 season.

Throughout the state the euphoria over the National Championship remained high during the off season. The team looked good in the spring practice, and there was a good deal of talk about repeating the feat in 1995. Realistically, however, the team had lost 14 of 22 starters off the '94 squad, and the offensive line, rated as possibly the best in Cornhusker history, had graduated, with the exception of center, Aaron Graham. True, Tommie Frazier was healthy once more, the stable of fine running backs, led by Lawrence Phillips was in tact, and the defense was thought to be talented. Consensus among the experts was that Nebraska would be good, but not great.

Coach Osborne might have described the 1995 season in the words of Charles Dickens: "It was the best of times. It was the worst of times". On the field the year started with a bang and continued to get better. The Huskers, behind Lawrence Phillips' 153 yards rushing and two touchdowns, completely dominated Oklahoma State 64-21. Again the next week the team romped past Michigan State 50-10. Once more Phillips had a fine game, 206 rushing yards and 3 touchdowns. After two weeks he had vaulted into the lead for the Heisman Trophy.

And as suddenly, Phillips' Heisman hopes evaporated. Late in the evening after the team returned from Lansing, Phillips broke into the apartment of a teammate and accosted his former girlfriend. He later turned himself into the police. Osborne immediately suspended Phillips from the team.

And so began, off the field, Osborne's "The worst of times".

The furor over his star running back's actions ignited women's groups throughout the country. No doubt the murder trial of O.J. Simpson contributed to the controversy, but the scrutiny of the public was intense. When Osborne decided to allow the University system to prevail in the case, he was perceived as coddling his athletes. When he readmitted Phillips to the team after a 6 game suspension he was accused of selling out his principles to "Win at all costs". When he tried to explain that he wanted to show compassion for his player as well as the girl, he was accused of duplicity.

An especially damaging report came from Bernard Goldberg of CBS, who had come to Lincoln to get an "unbiased story" about Phillips and some other Nebraska football players who had brushes with the law. In truth, he unleashed a hatchet job on "big time" football programs in general, and Nebraska and Coach Osborne in particular. That story, in one or another form, was told in most of the large newspapers throughout the country.

Coach Osborne did not back down through all the controversy. He monitored Phillips' punishment, which included counseling for anger control, and took pains to let the young man know that football and the team were still a part of his life.

It should be pointed out that not everyone had lost faith in Coach Osborne, his reputation of good sportsmanship, his Christian values, and his service to his fellow man. This reputation he had cultivated throughout his lifetime, and during his long tenure as a Nebraska coach. In Nebraska the consensus sentiment was solidly behind the coach's judgement. During this time Coach Osborne was presented two national awards.

In receiving the Father Flanagan Award for Service to Youth, Coach Osborne joined previous recipients, Mother Theresa, Jonas Saulk, and Denton Cooley, among others. He was also awarded the Distinguished American Award by The National Football Foundation and College Hall of Fame, given for Outstanding Contribution to Leadership, Betterment of Amateur Football, and Public Service. In this award he joined a select fraternity of past recipients, including Rev. Peter Hessberg, Vince Lombardi, Pete Rozelle and Bob Hope.

In the meantime, the Big Red Machine continued to roll on the field. Phillips was replaced by Clinton Childs in the backfield, who ran for 143 yards and two touchdowns in the 77-28 win over Arizona State. Damon Benning filled in for an injured Clinton Childs in the next game, against Pacific.. He ran for 173 yards and three touchdowns. The next week, against Washington State, it was Omaha freshman sensation Ahman Green's turn to shine, in a 176 yard, one touchdown game.

The Washington State game, 35-21, would prove to be the closest game of the season for the Cornhuskers. The defense came into its own in this game; And the offensive line proved to be in a class with the very best in Nebraska football history.

Through all of the troubles off the field the team remained focused on the goals that had been set---to win a 5th consecutive Big Eight Championship and to repeat as National Champions. Besides Coach Osborne's steadying influence, there was the strong senior leadership, exemplified by Aaron Graham, Christian Peter, and, above all, by quarterback, Tommie Frazier, who, as the season progressed, began to be touted for the Heisman trophy.

1995 was the year in which Athletic Director Bill Byrne's influence began to show. He overhauled the plan by which season tickets were awarded to long time ticket holders. Pressure was brought to bear on those ticket holders to make an extra donation to the athletic program for the privilege of having those tickets. The licensing of products carrying the Husker logo was revamped. Representatives from the University were sent out into the state to generate interest, and dollars, for the football program. There was considerable praise for Byrne's financial genius when the Athletic Department was able to report that its debt had been wiped out. There was also considerable grumbling over what many considered Byrne's strong arm tactics in raising money. This grumbling turned into a roar of indignation when Byrne announced that he was discarding Herbie Husker as the official mascot, citing a poor image nationwide for the Country Bumpkin mascot with the big red "N" on his overalls. People who had never even thought about Herbie Husker now came to his defense, and petitions from Omaha to Scottsbluff were drawn up to "Save Herbie from Oblivion". The outcry was heard in Lincoln, and, after just a short suspension, Herbie returned to the sidelines-- this time attired in football pants and a red "N" emblazoned jersey.

After another rout against Missouri, 57-0, there was some speculation that the Nebraska team might be something special, balanced by the thought that all of the teams played so far were just plain bad. When the

Huskers continued to roll over #8 Kansas State, 49-25, the perception began to grow that the team was playing at a higher level than anyone else. This thought grew the next week against #7 Colorado when the offense committed no penalties and no turnovers. Behind Frazier's best passing game, the Huskers continued the victory string, 44-25.

After Iowa State, 73-14, Nebraska routed #10 Kansas 41-3. The Huskers had soundly defeated three top 10 teams in four weeks by an average score of 45-16.

It was fitting that the final Big Eight game, before that league was discarded for the expanded Big 12 league, was played between the two all-time dominating teams of the Big Eight, Nebraska and Oklahoma. By this time Tommie Frazier had risen to one of the top candidates for the Heisman Trophy. The game was not one of the classics in this series, but as usual, Oklahoma's defense was strong. Unfortunately, Tommie Frazier's game was the least impressive of the year. The Husker defense more than rose to the occasion, however, and Nebraska prevailed, 37-0.

The game, none-the-less, had an adverse effect on Frazier's Heisman chances. When the trophy was awarded, (before the bowl games) Frazier finished 2nd in the balloting to Ohio State's Eddie George.

When Ohio State was defeated by Michigan late in the season, the stage was set for a show down in the Tostito Fiesta Bowl between #1 Nebraska and #2 Florida. The match-up was classic, Osborne's powerful, stodgy(?), running team, and Steve Spurrier's speedy, flashy, passing team. Speculation abounded, both ways, as to which system would prevail.

239

One very interesting dialogue went on for sometime on ESPN, where Lee Corso and Craig James expounded at length over the fact that Nebraska was not used to playing on a natural grass surface; therefore Super Gater Quarterback, Danny Wuerffel, would be able to have his way with the Husker secondary defenders. When it was pointed out that Nebraska had beaten Miami the year before, on grass, Corso's retort was, "That was Miami! This Florida team, my friend, is 25 times better than Miami of a year ago!"

And so, after all of the rhetoric, it came down to Nebraska vs Florida in the Fiesta Bowl. This time Frazier saved his best for last, as did the entire Cornhusker team. With the nationwide TV audience in shock, and Florida in disbelief, the Huskers methodically dismantled the Florida Gaters 62-24. The Florida running game was completely shut down, yielding a net -28 yards for the game. This enabled Charlie McBride's Husker defense to concentrate on disrupting Wuerffel's passing game. Wuerffel, who had been sacked only 10 times in 11 previous games was sacked 7 times, and threw 3 interceptions. The NU defense also recovered one fumble and accounted for nine points. Florida finished with 269 total yards, including just 14 in the fourth quarter.

Offensively, the Huskers played at peak efficiency. Lawrence Phillips, starting for the first time since his suspension, was at his early season form. His 165 yard, 2 touchdown game would have surely won the Most Valuable Player award had it not been for Tommie Frazier's finest game of a storied career. He threw for 105 yards and one touchdown, albeit with two interceptions. But he also ran for 199 yards and two touchdowns. In the third quarter Frazier uncorked a run which will surely be mentioned in the same class as the historic runs of Bobby Reynolds and Johnny Rodgers, Frazier ran through the entire Florida team, was touched by seven defenders, but kept his feet and scored from 75 yards out, a Nebraska Bowl record.

The game ended with third string quarterback Matt Turman kneeling at the Florida three yard line to let the clock run out.

The final year of the Big Eight ended on a very positive note. There were four Big Eight teams who ended the season with at least 10 wins, Nebraska, Colorado, Kansas State, and Kansas. All of these teams had won their bowl games with blow-outs, and all ended ranked in the top 10 in the country.

For The University of Nebraska it was a banner year. The football team ended up #1. The volleyball team captured the #1 ranking, and the Husker Marching Band was chosen as the #1 Marching Band in the country. A remarkable achievement! (Even the NU basketball team came to life. After a disastrous February, in which they lost 10 of their last 11 games and held a widely publicized walkout from practice, protesting Coach Nee's harsh methods, they rose up like Lazarus, in the NIT tournament. Playing all their games on the road, except the Washington State game, they won Nebraska's first ever national basketball tournament by defeating St. Joseph's of Pennsylvania 60-56 in New York's Madison Square Garden.)

Already there is speculation about the team's chances to bring off a "Three-Peat", and anticipation for spring practice to begin, so we can see what the

"Post-Frazier Era" will bring. As Coach Osborne found out long ago, the Husker fans are not satisfied with anything less than perfection.

April 1996

As this book was going to press the news broke that Brook Berringer, the selfless back-up quarterback on both the 1994 and 1995 Championship teams had been killed in an airplane accident just north of Lincoln on April 19th. This happened one day before the giant celebration was scheduled at Memorial Stadium to honor the NU National Championship Football team, the NU National Championship Volleyball team and the Nation's Number 1 Collegiate Marching Band.

The celebration was cancelled, leaving the state to grieve over the loss of this fine young man, and reflect on his heroic accomplishments during the 1994 season when he led the Nebraska team to victories despite a collapsed lung and other injuries, and even more, how he set an example as the ultimate team player while playing mostly in the shadow of Tommy Frazier.

To order additional copies of
GROWING UP IN PLAIN VIEW, complete the
information below.

Ship to: (please print)

Name_____

Address_____

City, State, Zip_____

Phone_____

_____copies of **GROWING UP IN PLAIN VIEW**

                     @$10 EACH_____
Nebraska residents
add 50 cents per book_____

Handling and shipping
         per order   <u>$2.50</u>

     total amount enclosed $_____

 Make checks payable to:
        GROWING UP IN PLAIN VIEW

Send to: **GROWING UP IN PLAIN VIEW**
      401 E. 1st St.
      Dept BK
      McCook, Nebraska 69001